THE CLEANEST RACE

THE CLEANEST RACE

How North Koreans See Themselves—And Why It Matters

B. R. MYERS

 MELVILLEHOUSE
BROOKLYN, NEW YORK

THE CLEANEST RACE
© 2010 B.R. Myers

First Melville House printing: December 2009

Melville House Publishing
145 Plymouth Street
Brooklyn, NY 11201

www.mhpbooks.com

ISBN: 978-1-933633-91-6

Book design by Kelly Blair

Printed in the United States of America

Library of Congress Cataloging-in-Publication Data

Myers, B. R., 1963-
 The cleanest race : how North Koreans see themselves and why it matters
/ B.R. Myers.—1st ed.
   p. cm.
 ISBN 978-1-933633-91-6
 1. Korea (North)—Social conditions. 2. Propaganda, North Korean—
Social aspects. 3. Nationalism—Korea (North) 4. National characteristics,
Korean. 5. Ethnicity—Korea (North) I. Title.
 HN730.6.Z9M66 2010
 303.3'75095193—dc22
                                    2009045072

CONTENTS

11 **PREFACE**

23 **PART I**
    A History of North Korea's Official Culture

69 **PART II**
    Understanding North Korea Through Its Myths

71 **Mother Korea and Her Children**
93 **The Parent Leader**
111 **The Dear Leader**
129 **Foreigners**
151 **The Yankee Colony**

163 **CONCLUSION**

171 **NOTES**
191 **BIBLIOGRAPHY**

MOTHER: 1) The woman who has given birth to one: *Father and mother; a mother's love. A mother's benevolence is higher than a mountain, deeper than the ocean.* Also used in the sense of "a woman who has a child": *What all mothers anxiously want is for their children to grow up healthy and become magnificent red builders.* 2) A respectful term for someone of an age similar to one's own mother: *Comrade Platoon Leader called Dŏngmani's mother "mother" and always helped her in her work.* 3) A metaphor for being loving, looking after everything, and worrying about others: *Party officials must become mothers who ceaselessly love and teach the Party rank and file, and become standard-bearers at the forefront of activities. In other words, someone in charge of lodgings has to become a mother to the boarders. This means looking carefully after everything: whether someone is cold or sick, how they are eating, and so on.* 4) A metaphor for the source from which something originates: *The Party is the great mother of everything new. Necessity is the mother of invention.*

FATHER: the husband of one's birth mother.

Two entries from a North Korean dictionary of the Korean language, 1964

PREFACE

The most important questions regarding North Korea are the ones least often asked: What do the North Koreans believe? How do they see themselves and the world around them? Yes, we know the country has a personality cult, but this fact alone tells us little. Cuba has a personality cult too, yet the Castro regime espouses an ideology quite different from that of its counterpart in Pyongyang. On what grounds is the North Korean Leader so extravagantly acclaimed? What is the nature of his mission, and the purported destiny of his nation as a whole? Only through this sort of information can one begin to make sense of the Democratic People's Republic of Korea (DPRK), to use its formal name. It is unfortunate but by no means surprising that our news correspondents eschew such topics in order to return *ad nauseum* to the same monuments and mass games, the same girl directing traffic. More remarkable has been the extent to which academics, think-tank analysts and other Pyongyang watchers have neglected to study the worldview of the military-first regime. Regardless of their own political leanings (and North Korean studies remains marked by a sharp left-right divide), they have tended toward interpretations of the country in which ideology plays next to no role. Conservatives generally explain the dictatorship's behavior in terms of a cynical struggle to maintain power and privilege, while liberals prefer to regard the DPRK as a "rational actor," a country behaving much as any tiny country would in the face of a hostile superpower. Such interest as either camp can bring to bear on so-called soft issues exhausts itself in futile attempts to make sense of Juche Thought, a sham doctrine with no bearing on Pyongyang's policy-making.

To be sure, the Western world is generally much less interested in ideology—for reasons that are themselves ideological—than it was during the Cold War. Most Americans know just as little about Islamism as they did before 9/11. But why is there more talk of ideological matters in any issue of *Arab Studies Journal* than in a dozen issues of *North Korean Review*? The obvious if undiplomatic answer is that most Pyongyang watchers do not understand Korean well enough to read the relevant official texts. But even scholars with the requisite language skills would rather research other topics, usually of a military, nuclear or economic nature. One colleague told me he finds the North Korean personality cult too absurd to take seriously; indeed, he doubts whether even the leadership believes it. But no regime would go to such enormous expense, year in, year out for sixty years, to inculcate into its citizens a worldview to which it did not itself subscribe. (The only institution in the country that did not miss a beat during the famine of the mid-1990s was the propaganda apparatus.) As for absurdity: the examples of Nazi Germany and Pol Pot's Cambodia show that a dictator and his subjects are capable of believing and acting upon ideas far more ridiculous than anything ever espoused by the Workers' Party. For all the hyperbole in which it is couched, and the histrionics with which it is proclaimed, North Korean propaganda is not nearly as outlandish as the uninitiated think. No matter what some American Christian groups might claim, divine powers have never been attributed to either of the two Kims. In fact, the propaganda apparatus in Pyongyang has generally been careful *not* to make claims that run directly counter to its citizens' experience or common sense. Granted, it has made museum exhibits out of chairs that Kim Il Sung rested on while visiting this factory or that farm, but there is no reason to doubt that he actually *did* sit on the things. (In most cases there is an authenticating photograph nearby.) This approach can be contrasted with that of Stalin's Soviet Union, or Mao's China, where propagandists were not quite so effusive or incessant in their praise of the leader, yet regularly made claims—of bumper harvests, for example—which everyone knew to be untrue.

While ignoring North Korean ideology, the West has assiduously, almost compulsively, added to its pile of "hard" information on the country. Much of this has come from experts in nuclear or economic studies. Aid workers have also contributed accounts of their experiences in the country. An international network of Google Earth users is busily identifying structures visible in aerial photographs.¹ Despite all this, experts continue to describe North Korea as "puzzling," "baffling," a "mystery"—and no wonder. Hard facts cannot be put to proper use unless one first acquires information of a very different nature. If we did not know that Iran is an Islamic country, it would forever baffle us, no matter how good the rest of our intelligence might be.

Unfortunately a lack of relevant expertise has never prevented observers from mischaracterizing North Korean ideology to the general public. They call the regime "hard-line communist" or "Stalinist," despite its explicit racial theorizing, its strident acclamation of Koreans as the world's "cleanest" or "purest" race. They describe it as a Confucian patriarchy, despite its maternal authority figures, or as a country obsessed with self-reliance, though it has depended on outside aid for over sixty years. By far the most common mistake, however, has been the projection of Western or South Korean values and common sense onto the North Koreans. For example: Having been bombed flat by the Americans in the 1950s, the DPRK *must* be fearful for its security, ergo it *must* want the normalization of relations with Washington.

These various fallacies have combined to make the West worry less about North Korea's nuclear program than about Iran's. The word Confucianism makes us think of Singapore, Asian whiz-kids, and respect for the elderly; how much trouble can a Confucian patriarchy be? Self-reliance does not sound too dangerous either. Communism has a much less benign ring to it, of course, but if there is one thing we remember from the Cold War, it is that it ended peacefully. For fifteen years the perception of a communist North Korea has sustained the US government's hope that disarmament talks will work with Pyongyang as they did with Moscow. Only in 2009, after the Kim Jong Il regime defied the United Nations by launching a ballistic missile and conducting its second underground nuclear test, did a consensus begin to emerge that negotiations were unlikely ever to work. Yet the assumption prevails that the worst Pyongyang would ever do is sell nuclear material or expertise to more dangerous forces in the Middle East. All the while the military-first regime has been invoking kamikaze slogans last used by imperial Japan in the Pacific War.

In this book, therefore, I aim to explain North Korea's dominant ideology or worldview—I use the words inter-changeably—and to show how far removed it is from communism, Confucianism *and* the show-window doctrine of Juche Thought. Far from complex, it can be summarized in a single sentence: *The Korean people are too pure blooded, and therefore too virtuous, to survive in this evil world without a great parental leader.* More must be added perhaps, if only to explain that "therefore" to an American reader, but not much more of importance. I need hardly point out that if such a race-based worldview is to be situated on our conventional left-right spectrum, it makes more sense to posit it on the extreme right than on the far left. Indeed, the similarity to the worldview of fascist Japan is striking. I do not, however, intend to label North Korea as fascist, a term too vague to be much use. It is enough for me to make clear that the country has always been, at the very least, ideologically closer to America's adversaries in World War II than to communist China and Eastern Europe. This truth alone, if properly grasped, will not only help the West to understand the loyalty shown to the DPRK by its chronically impoverished citizens, but also to understand why the West's policy of pursuing late Cold War-type solutions to the nuclear problem is doomed to fail.

The word ideology is used in this book in accordance with Martin Seliger's understanding of it, which Zeev Sternhell puts in the following nutshell: "a conceptual frame of reference which provides criteria for choice and decision by virtue of which the major activities of an organized community are governed."[2] Note the word *major*. No ideology determines every aspect of a nation's daily life. Technology, production and administration have always been guided in the DPRK by what Franz Schurmann referred to, in regard to China, as the "practical ideology of expertise."[3] And like all parties, the Workers' Party is ready to resort to temporary deviations from ideological essentials in order to maintain its hold on power. Paranoid, race-based nationalism has nonetheless guided the DPRK in its policy-making from the start. It is only in this ideological context that the country's distinguishing characteristics—which the outside world, with its Stalinist-Confucian model, has always found so baffling—make perfect sense.

What is more, this ideology has generally enjoyed the support of the North Korean people through good times and bad. Even today, with a rival state thriving next door, the regime is able to maintain public stability without a ubiquitous police presence or a fortified northern border. Sensationalist American accounts of the "underground railroad" helping North Korean "refugees" make it through China to the free world gloss over the fact that about half of these economic migrants—for that is what most of them are—*voluntarily return* to their homeland. The rest remain fervent admirers of Kim Il Sung if not of his son. Though we must never forget the men, women and children languishing in Yodŏk and other prison camps, we cannot keep carrying on as if the dictatorship did not enjoy a significant degree of mass support. How significant? Enough to make the regime desperate to hold on to it. I intend to argue, however, that this support cannot be sustained for long, because what the masses are taught—especially in regard to South Korean public opinion—is coming increasingly into conflict with what they know to be true. It is the regime's awareness of a pending legitimacy crisis, not a fear of attack from without, which makes it behave ever more provocatively on the world stage.

The official worldview is not set out coherently in the leaders' writings. These are more often praised than read.[4] So-called Juche Thought functions at most as an imposing row of book-spines, a prop in the personality cult. (A good way to embarrass one's minders in the DPRK is to ask them to explain it.) Unlike Soviet citizens under Stalin, or Chinese under Mao, North Koreans learn more about their leaders than from them.[5] It is not in ideological treatises but in the more mass-oriented domestic propaganda that the official worldview is expressed most clearly and unselfconsciously. I stress the word *domestic*. Too many observers wrongly assume that the (North) Korean Central News Agency's English-language releases reflect the same sort of propaganda that the home audience gets. In fact there are significant differences. For example, where the DPRK presents itself to the outside world as a misunderstood country seeking integration into the international community, it presents itself to its own citizens (as I will show later) as a rogue state that breaks agreements with impunity, dictates conditions to groveling U.N. officials, and keeps its enemies in constant fear of ballistic retribution. Generally speaking the following rule of thumb applies: the less accessible a propaganda outlet is to the outside world, the blunter and more belligerent it will be in its expression of the racist orthodoxy.

The following chapters are based on my own extensive research of as many different forms of domestic propaganda as I could find at the Unification Ministry's North Korea Resource Center in Seoul. (This is, ironically enough, a better place to study the stuff than Pyongyang, where a foreigner's requests for anything more than a few months old are met with suspicion.)[6] From nightly news reports and television dramas to animated cartoons and war movies; from the white-papered *Rodong Sinmun*, the Workers' Party organ, to women's and children's magazines printed on rough, gray paper; from short stories and historical novels to dictionaries, encyclope-diae and school textbooks (these last printed, semi-legibly, on the worst paper of all); from reproductions of wall posters, oil paintings and caricatures to photographs of monuments and statues: these are the sources I have spent much of the past eight years studying.[7] In the interest of brevity and vari-ation—and in emulation of Alfred Pfabigan's practice in a perceptive travelogue entitled *Schlaflos in Pjöngjang* (1986)—I will occasionally refer to the body of myths espoused in this propaganda as the Text, though the reader is not, of course, to imagine a closed set of books.

Why would such a secretive country export propaganda that lays bare the true nature of its official ideology? There are many reasons. One is that the DPRK has never relinquished its dream of fomenting a nationalist revolution in South Korea. Another is that it can earn hard currency by selling these materials at a high price to one or two licensed distributors, who in turn sell them to research libraries abroad. Perhaps most importantly, the regime rightly assumes that almost no one hostile to the DPRK will ever bother to look at these materials. (I can count on one hand the times I ever saw a Western visitor take a North Korean book from the Resource Center's shelves.) Finally, and unfortunately, the more sensitive content is kept out of mass-produced, "hard copy" propaganda and confined to outlets intended exclusively for domestic eyes and ears. A current example is the on-again, off-again glorification of Kim Jong Il's putative successor Kim Jong Ŭn, a mainly oral campaign carried out at party lectures, factory assemblies and the like, and through unprepossessing posters hung in display cases far from tourist sites. Fortunately a sharp-eyed Taiwanese business traveler managed to photograph one of these posters, thus affording the outside world some insight into the nature of this budding personality cult. Regardless of whether Kim Jong Ŭn actually ends up taking power, I regret not having been able to include more about his myth in these pages.

* * *

This book is divided into two parts. The first recounts the historical development of the official culture, starting with

its origins in colonial Korea. In the second part I will discuss each of the Text's main myths in turn, from those of the
Korean child race and its motherly leaders to the myth of
the "Yankee colony" to the south. Each chapter in part two
contains an italicized section in which I take the liberty of
condensing the relevant myth to a page or two, telling it sans
excursions and in strict chronological order—admittedly, a
very un- Korean thing to do. This way the reader can check the
main assertions of anti-American propaganda, say, without
necessarily having to bother with my ensuing evaluation of it.
(These sections were written with a view to the many people
who have complained to me about the unreadable diffuseness
and repetitiveness of the few North Korean books available
in English.) Although I have written these sections in a prose
meant to replicate the effusiveness of the original propaganda,
I do not want anyone mistaking them for direct quotes; hence
the italics.

   In closing, let me make perfectly clear that in this book
(if not in my last book on North Korean culture) I am
more interested in thematic content than aesthetic form.[8]
I also focus more on propaganda that sheds light on North
Korea's relationship to the outside world than on propaganda
regarding, say, the land reclamation project. If this constitutes
"essentializing," to use a trendy pejorative, so be it. Anyone
interested in a discussion of the DPRK's literature as literature, or art as art, is advised to look elsewhere. So too are
readers who want to know how the propaganda apparatus is
organized, how the broadcast networks operate, and so on.

   The McCune-Reischauer system is used throughout this
book, with the customary exceptions for names (e.g. Kim Il

Sung) and words (e.g. juche) better known in other spell-
ings. Finally, I would like to thank Dongseo University for
supporting my research, and Ms Eunjeong Lee for helping me
track down certain North Korean materials. Responsibility
for all errors in this book is mine.

B.R. Myers, Busan, South Korea, October 2009

PART I

A History of North Korea's Official Culture

CHAPTER ONE
THE COLONIAL ERA, 1910-1945

Korean schoolchildren in North and South learn that Japan invaded their fiercely patriotic country in 1905, spent forty years trying to destroy its language and culture, and withdrew without having made any significant headway. This version of history is just as uncritically accepted by most foreigners who write about Korea. Yet the truth is more complex. For much of the country's long history its northern border was fluid, and the national identities of literate Koreans and Chinese mutually indistinguishable.[1] Believing their civilization to have been founded by a Chinese sage in China's image, educated

Koreans subscribed to a Confucian worldview that posited their country in a position of permanent subservience to the Middle Kingdom. Even when Korea isolated itself from the mainland in the seventeenth century, it did so in the conviction that it was guarding Chinese tradition better than the Chinese themselves. For all their xenophobia, therefore, the Koreans were no nationalists. As Carter Eckert has written, "There was little, if any, feeling of loyalty toward the abstract concept of Korea as a nation-state, or toward fellow inhabitants of the peninsula as 'Koreans.'"[2] It was not until the late nineteenth century, and under Japanese sponsorship, that a reform-minded cabinet undertook measures to establish Korea's independence and imbue the people with a sense of national pride.

The Japanese freed the peninsula from China only to take it for themselves. In 1905 Tokyo established a protectorate over Korea, assuming control first of its foreign, then its domestic affairs. Annexation of the peninsula followed in 1910. Public opposition to Japanese rule grew until patriots read out a declaration of independence on March 1, 1919 in Seoul, setting off a nationwide uprising. The authorities responded with a brutal show of force before relaxing some of the repressive policies that had inflamed their subjects.

Although nationalists took advantage of new Korean-language newspapers to canvas support, they were no match for the colonial propaganda machine, which now sought to co-opt Korean pride instead of stamping it out. It asserted that Koreans shared the same ancient progenitor, bloodline and benevolent ruler as the Japanese themselves; both peoples thus belonged to one "imperial" race morally (if not physically and intellectually) superior to all others.[3] The dominant slogan of the day was *naisen ittai* or "Interior [i.e. Japan] and Korea as one body." While intent on undermining their subjects' sense of a distinct nationhood, the authorities emphasized that *naisen ittai* did not mean the end of Koreanness, and even posed as champions of a culture that had languished too long in China's shadow. Koreans were encouraged to cherish their "region" and its "dialect," even its yin-yang flag (which was printed in school maps and atlases right up to liberation), as long as they remembered that the peninsula was but one part of a greater Japanese whole.[4]

A postcard from the "Japan and Korea as one body" campaign of the 1930s shows Japan (r) and its colony as schoolboy partners, running a three-legged race over the globe.

Nationalist intellectuals attempted to counter this propaganda by reviving interest in the legend of Tan'gun. Set down in an anthology of folk-tales in 1284, then largely ignored for centuries, it told how this half-divine figure had inaugurated the first Korean kingdom with his seed in 2333 BC. As the nationalists saw it, the tale gave the Koreans their own pure bloodline, a civilization grounded in a unique culture, and over four millennia of history to their colonizers' three. One writer even tried to establish Mount Paektu, a volcanic mountain on the border with China, as Tan'gun's birthplace and a counterpart to Japan's sacred Mount Fuji.[5] The South Korean historian Yi Yŏng-hun puts it best: "The myths and symbols needed to form a nation were coined new in the awareness of Japan's myths and symbols—in opposition to and in emulation of them."[6] The public proved indifferent to this derivative mythmaking, however, and by the end of the 1930s most prominent nationalists had themselves become enthusiastic advocates of the new order.

Korea's left-wing writers executed a similar *volte face*. Rounded up and imprisoned in the early 1930s, then released after promising to behave themselves, they soon began lending their voices to the great militarist chorus. As the Korean-language *Maeil sinbo* newspaper remarked with satisfaction in 1944, writers of all ideological stripes—communist, nationalist, libertarian—had united in support for the system.[7]

But even while these writers glorified the emperor, they urged their countrymen to cherish their Koreanness.[8] In romance novels frail Japanese women fell in love with strong Korean men, much as they still do in South Korean films and dramas.[9] Illustrations in newspapers and magazines showed girls in traditional *hanbok* costume waving the Japanese flag, and Confucian gentlemen in horsehair hats standing proudly by their newly recruited sons.[10] The regime stimulated pride in "peninsular" history for imperial ends, encouraging Koreans to reclaim their ancient territory by settling in Manchuria.[11] One writer invoked the elite *hwarang* soldiers of the Silla dynasty to whip up fighting spirit.[12] Another called on young men to "demonstrate the loyalty of a Japanese citizen and the spirit of a son of Korea" by volunteering to fight in the "holy war" against the Yankees.[13] As the historian Cho Kwan-ja has remarked, these collaborators regarded themselves as "pro-Japanese [Korean] nationalists."[14]

Little of this propaganda reached the illiterate majority of the population, who often had to be brutally coerced into complying with Japanese demands for soldiers, laborers and prostitutes.[15] The educated classes, however, being more highly propagandized (as the educated always are), and enjoying the benefits of the new order, generally behaved as the authorities wanted them to. Granted, a repressive system was in place.[16] But one must either assume that the average educated Korean harbored a fierce opposition to the *status quo*, and collaborated in painful awareness of his fear and hypocrisy, or that he chose to believe he was serving his people as part of a winning racial team. No one familiar with human nature can doubt that the latter assumption is more likely to be true.[17] It is borne out by evidence of widespread over-compliance with the *naisen ittai* campaign. By the end of the 1920s the upper and middle classes in Seoul were speaking Japanese in their own homes.[18] Marriages between Koreans and their colonizers were, as a famous short story later put it, "thought quite natural by many, perhaps even a mark of distinction."[19] (In South Korea, marriage with Japanese citizens remains the form of international marriage with the least social stigma attached.) Newsreels of the imperial army's victories in the Pacific War elicited vigorous applause from moviegoers.[20]

They had less to clap about as the war progressed. By early 1945 propaganda had taken on a note of desperation. "If our destiny is thwarted in this war...it would be a tragedy for all mankind," the Korean-language daily warned in March. "We must win."[21] But on August 6 the atomic bomb was dropped on Hiroshima, emboldening the USSR to enter the war with Japan. The Red Army was advancing swiftly down the Korean peninsula on August 15 when Hirohito read out his famous surrender notice. By that time the US and the Soviet Union had already decided, without consulting the Koreans themselves, to share the administration of the former Japanese colony for an indefinite period. The Red Army occupied the north, setting up headquarters for a so-called Soviet Civil Administration in the ancient city of Pyongyang. American soldiers arrived in September to take over Seoul and the rest of the southern half of the peninsula.[22]

THE SOVIET OCCUPATION, 1945-1948

Though most Koreans in 1945 had no memory of life before Japanese rule, neither the Soviets nor the Americans saw a need to de-colonize hearts and minds. That the Koreans now hated Japan was taken as proof that they had always done so. Nor did either power punish former propagandists. In Seoul, the cultural scene's spontaneous efforts to come to terms with its past were soon undermined by the settling of personal scores and a general refusal to acknowledge a collective guilt.[1] Obscure ex-collaborators condemned the famous ones, those who had propagandized in Korean asserted moral superiority over those who had done so in Japanese, and erstwhile "proletarians" acted as if their brief prison stays in the 1930s made up for everything they had written afterward.

Meanwhile, to the north, the Soviet authorities set about orchestrating a "people's revolution" of the kind already underway in much of Eastern Europe. The first stage was to be a coalition between communists and other forces, followed by a pseudo-coalition in which the communists called the shots, and finally a monolithic regime.[2] This plan was complicated by the lack of left-wingers in the north of the country, which had hitherto been a bastion of conservatives and Christians. The occupying power had to build up a local party from scratch while courting right-wing partners for a coalition.[3] For all their feigned impartiality, the Soviets lost no time transferring ownership of printing presses, publishing houses and radio stations to the fledgling Workers' Party. The first issue of the party daily (known today as the *Rodong sinmun*) appeared in September 1945.[4] The radio network began operations on

October 14, 1945 by broadcasting a mass rally in Pyongyang to honor the Soviet liberators.[5]

Among the Koreans who took the podium that day was Kim Il Sung, a Pyongyang-born thirty-three-year-old who had attained the rank of captain in the Red Army. Although Kim had sat out the Pacific War in the USSR, he had earlier fought against the Japanese as a commander in Mao Zedong's army, acquiring brief renown in 1937 for an attack on an imperial outpost just south of the Yalu River.[6] For better or worse Kim was the closest thing to a resistance fighter the Koreans had. He is said to have wanted a military career, but the Soviets, finding no more appropriate person to work with, persuaded him to assume leadership of the new state. Yet Kim was by far the least educated of all the leaders in the socialist world. His spotty schooling had ended at seventeen, and although he had spent a year at an infantry officer school in the USSR, it is unlikely that he understood enough Russian to grasp anything theoretical. None of his writings evinces an understanding of Marx.[†] Equally ignorant of communist ideology were the guerilla comrades who comprised the core of Kim's power base. Andrei Lankov, a prominent Korea researcher, has written that "with the exception of the Soviet Koreans, no top cadres had undergone training in… Marxism-Leninism."[7] It is no wonder that instead of guiding the cultural scene in ideological matters the party allowed itself to be guided by it.

Contrary to South Korean left-wing myth, which the American historian Bruce Cumings has done much to nurture, almost all intellectuals who moved to Pyongyang after liberation had collaborated with the Japanese to some

Kim Il Sung

[†] I once spoke to a German lady, a Korea scholar, who had interpreted for Kim during his visit to East Berlin. Though an admirer of the man, she conceded, "He seemed never to have read a serious book."

degree. Several who had done so with special enthusiasm, like the novelist Kim Sa-ryang, had been virtually run out of Seoul. The North was *more* and not less hospitable to such collaborators. As a history book published in the DPRK in 1981 puts it, "the Great Leader Kim Il Sung refuted the mistaken tendency to doubt or ostracize people just because they...had worked for Japanese institutions in the past."[8] Kim's own brother, it is worth remembering, had interpreted for Japanese troops in China.[9]

From one Great Marshal on a white horse to another; Hirohito (above) and Kim Il Sung (below) atop their respective purity symbols. Kim Jong Il, here on his father's arm, has been filmed and photographed on white horses of his own.

But retaining the emperor's administrators and techno-crats was one thing, and retaining his propagandists another—or so one would have thought. According to Marxism-Leninism, a communist party's main task lies in infusing the masses with revolutionary consciousness.[10] It is remarkable, therefore, that when the North Korean Federation of Literature and Art was established in March 1946, most of the top posts went to well-known veterans of the wartime cultural apparatus, like the playwright Song Yŏng and the choreographer Ch'oi Sŭng-hŭi.[11] No writer was excluded from the party or its cultural organizations due to pro-Japanese activities, let alone imprisoned for them (as Yi Kwang-su and Ch'oi Nam-sŏn were in Seoul).

The Workers' Party had to wait until 1948 to receive its own crash course in Marxism-Leninism and was therefore unable to provide much guidance to writers and artists.[12] Reading out a speech crudely plagiarized from Mao, Kim Il Sung told them to study Marxism and "communicate with the masses in words they understand."[13] A Soviet-Korean poet took it upon himself to regale admiring fellow writers with a list of socialist realist classics not yet translated into Korean.[14] Other than that, the party simply doled out themes, starting in early 1946 with that of land reform. None of the literati wanted to make the first move. "How was one to write a novel or poem on land reform?... All put their heads to one side, finally concluding it was an impossible task."[15] Only when the party responded angrily to an anthology of love poems in January 1947 did North Korean writers begin propagandizing in earnest.[16]

Not surprisingly, their work bore the influence of the ideology they had spent much of their lives disseminating. Having been ushered by the Japanese into the world's purest race, the Koreans in 1945 simply kicked the Japanese out of it. The legend of the ancient racial progenitor Tan'gun, which Korean nationalists had failed to popularize during the 1920s, came almost overnight to be regarded as historical truth. Japanese symbols were transposed into Korean ones. Mount Paektu, hitherto known only as the peninsula's highest peak, suddenly attained a Fuji-like, sacral status as the presumed place of Tan'gun's birth.[17] Much of the Japanese version of Korean history—from its blanket condemnation of Chinese influence to its canards about murderous Yankee missionaries—was carried over whole. This is not to say that North Korean ideology simply codified what everyone already believed. The average illiterate citizen was likely no more nationalist in 1945 than he had been in 1910. It was the Japanese-schooled minority which now put a radio in every village, taught the peasants to read, sent children to school— and convinced the race that it was the purest in the world.

Gone, however, was the confident tone of imperial propaganda. Where the colonial power had touted Japanese virtue as a protective talisman, the Koreans now believed that *their* virtue had made them as vulnerable as children to an evil world. What by international standards had been an enviably placid history was now remembered as a long litany of suffering and humiliation at foreign hands. In depictions of the colonial era, novelists and painters focused on the forced labor of little girls and boys, thus reinforcing the impression of a child race abused by an adult one.[18] Because Koreans truly were as the perfidious Japanese had only claimed to be, i.e. inherently virtuous, never evil by nature, all atrocities they had committed during the Pacific War were ascribed to duress and quickly erased from the collective memory.[19] Koreans had done nothing under the Japanese but suffer. [†]

The new racial self-image manifested itself clearly in stories of Soviet-Korean friendship written and published in the late 1940s.[20] Writers depicted ailing men and women being carried to hospitals on the backs of Russian nurses and female doctors. Lest anyone miss the symbolism, the heroines were explicitly compared to mothers, the locals to children.[21]

> Even in the hardest times Wŏnju had only to look into Dr. Kriblyak's eyes to know that he would not die. His heart was always in her embrace, as if he were being held at his mother's bosom.[22]

The genre was evidently meant to flatter the Soviets with the implication of filial subservience, and at the same time to plead for motherly protection of a race too pure to survive on its own. These tales should not, however, be misread as asserting the moral equality (let alone superiority) of the Russian people. Just as foreigners can be evil, while Koreans can only do it, so it is that only the child race is *inherently* virtuous; foreigners can at best do the occasional good deed.

The North Koreans were by no means alone in re-inventing their past, nor were they the only nationalists in the new East Bloc. The historian Tony Judt has written that myths of a "France of resisters or a Poland of victims" played an important role in helping Europe set aside its past and move on.[23] But there is an enormous difference between nationalism and a race-based view of the world. The North Koreans' image of themselves as inherently pure and vulnerable would prove particularly problematic, encouraging as it did both a dislike

[†] Much the same myth is propagated south of the DMZ. In 2006 a South Korean government commission announced that of eighty-six Koreans convicted by the Allies of war crimes, eighty-three should be regarded as blameless "victims of Japan." A telling exception was made for those who had committed crimes against other Koreans. Alford explores the Koreans' refusal to attribute evil to their country-men in *Think No Evil* (1999), but draws the wrong conclusion that they have no concept of evil at all.

of their allies *and* a chronic dependence on them.

This worldview also posed problems for iconographers of the new personality cult, for Kim Il Sung had to be presented on the one hand as the embodiment of Korean naivety and on the other as a brilliant revolutionary warrior. The logical solution would have been for the regime to re-conceive ethnic virtues so as to include the qualities of strength, discipline and wisdom. Attempting to do just that, the Soviet-Korean poet Cho Ki-ch˘on—one of the few intellectuals in Pyongyang who had not received a Japanese schooling—depicted Kim as a brilliant strategist who read Soviet history between battles.[24] Han Sŏr-ya and other homegrown writers and artists, however, acclaimed a nurturing, maternal leader, one whose success derived more from his naivety and innocence than anything else. He had mastered Marxism-Leninism with his heart, not his brain, and his best ideas came to him in his sleep.[25] It was this latter image that took hold, though the Soviet-Koreans are said to have found it as bizarre and comical as we in the West do today.[26]

Needless to say, no mention was made of the fact that "the General" had spent the Pacific War years in a rural Soviet

Kim Jong Il as a spartan, Juche-minded 18 year old, one of many images designed to counter the assumption that he had a care-free or privileged upbringing.

town. Instead he and his guerillas were said to have fought the occupying power from a secret base on Mount Paektu. This clever lie put the heroic troops just inside the homeland during the national ordeal while offering a plausible explanation as to why no one could remember seeing them. No less importantly, it linked Kim to Tan'gun's alleged birthplace.[27]

North Korea's personality cult quickly surpassed its Eastern European counterparts in extravagance. By the end of the 1940s the leading university had been named after the leader, his home village of Man'gyŏngdae had become a national shrine, and his statue had gone up in several cities. Unlike Stalin and Mao, Kim tolerated no sub-cults of the second or third in command; there was no one to compare with Beria or Lin Biao. By today's standards, however, the cult was still rather modest, conceding both the "great" Stalin's primacy and the Red Army's decisive role in liberating the peninsula. Nor were Kim's name and image quite as ubiquitous as they would later become.

Like the blood-based Japanese nationalism of the colonial era, the new Korean nationalism went hand in hand with the slavish imitation of foreign models and an often contemptuous indifference to indigenous traditions. In his speechifying Kim declared servile tribute to the USSR's "superior" culture.[28] Literary critics tossed around Soviet catchwords—"typicality," and so on—in an effort to cut down their rivals on the cultural scene. University students scrambled to learn Russian, the new linguistic ticket to social status. Meanwhile the Soviet Civil Administration rapidly expanded the fascist command economy of the Pacific War era into a communist one.[29]

To outside observers, therefore, North Korea gave every appearance of being another Soviet satellite in the making.

A portion of a mosaic in Pyongyang commemorating the triumphant homecoming.

But a closer look at the official culture would have revealed a different truth. Where East Bloc propagandists dwelled on the dialectical struggle between the old and the new, their North Korean counterparts presented their half of the peninsula as an already classless *gemeinschaft*, unanimously supportive of Kim Il Sung, under whose protective rule the child race could finally indulge its wholesome instincts. As in imperial Japanese propaganda, the dominant dualism was one of purity versus impurity, cleanliness versus filth.[30] Protagonists in official narratives were boyish young men and blushing, virginal girls. One novel of the period broke with convention by depicting the romance between a widower and the former concubine of a landowner. Kim Il Sung himself was quick to complain, saying that the widower should have been hitched up to a virgin instead. "Even an old maid would do," he grumbled. "Everyone wants pure water."[31]

One searches these early works in vain for a sense of fraternity with the world proletariat. The North Koreans saw no contradiction between regarding the USSR as developmentally superior on the one hand and morally inferior on the other. (The parallel to how South Koreans have always viewed the United States is obvious.) Efforts to keep this contempt a secret were undermined by over-confidence in the impenetrability of the Korean language and the inability of all nationalists to put themselves in a foreigner's shoes. The Workers' Party was taken by surprise, for example, when Red Army authorities objected to a story about a thuggish Soviet soldier who mends his ways after encountering a saintly Korean street urchin—another child character symbolizing the purity of the race.[32]

WAR AND RECONSTRUCTION, 1948-1966

On August 13, 1948 Syngman Rhee announced the establishment of the Republic of Korea (ROK), whereupon Soviet officials in Pyongyang, abandoning hopes for a single state, relinquished power to Kim Il Sung. The Democratic People's Republic of Korea (DPRK) was formally established on September 9. Having flown the same yin-yang symbol as the American zone for three years, the DPRK now hoisted a communist-style flag, with a red star as the focal point. At the end of 1948 Soviet troops withdrew from the peninsula. No sooner had they gone than Kim began enlisting Moscow's support for a military re-unification of the country. Stalin agreed to send weapons, supplies, and advisers.[1] Meanwhile the DPRK's propaganda apparatus prepared the masses for the coming conflict. The South had gone from a Japanese colonial hell to an American one, with the same treasonous elite in charge; how long would the suffering brethren have to wait for *real* liberation? Yi T'ae-chun and other writers wrote short stories or poems demanding violent retribution against the Yankees and their lackeys.[2]

On June 25, 1950 the Korean People's Army launched what would later be called the "Homeland Liberation War" with a surprise advance across the 38th parallel.[†] Capturing Seoul on June 28, KPA troops rolled as far south as the Nakdong River before MacArthur's landing in September at Inch'ŏn, a harbor city on the west coast, reversed the course of the war. As UN soldiers neared Pyongyang, the cultural apparatus joined the party leadership in fleeing north. China entered the war in October, pushing the Americans and their allies back down

[†]Although the North Koreans refer to the Korean War in English-language propaganda as the Fatherland Liberation War, they refer to Korea in their own language as the Homeland or Motherland (literally Mother Homeland). See the following chapters for more on the DPRK's penchant for mother metaphors.

the peninsula. Seoul was recaptured by the communists only to fall once again to UN troops, in whose hands it remained. Kim's writers and artists then hunkered down in a village near Pyongyang while the US Air Force embarked on a long and indiscriminate bombing campaign.

Such a war would have brought out the xenophobia in any nation, but in the DPRK, where most people had been steeped in blood-based nationalism since their colonial childhood, the mood was such that even the Chinese ally was regarded with hostility.[3] Writers depicted the Americans, including women and children, as an inherently depraved race.[4] There was none of the proletarian internationalism that had made Soviet propagandists draw a line between Nazis and average Germans. One writer jeered at the corpses of UN troops, while another celebrated the abuse of captured enemy pilots.[5] Much sport was made of the Yankees' Caucasian features, with a leading author asserting that they reflected an inner "idiotization."[6] The same man also penned a short story named *Jackals* (Sŭngnyangi, 1951) in which US missionaries murder a Korean child with an injection of germs.[7] The enormous popularity of this story may well have inspired the regime in late 1951 to make formal allegations of American germ warfare.

In 1952 a war-weary Kim Il Sung called on China to help bring about a ceasefire. Mao and Stalin both urged him to stand firm.[8] After the generalissimo's death in May 1953, Moscow at last permitted Kim to enter into negotiations with the enemy. The DPRK and China signed an armistice with the United States on July 27, 1953. Pyongyang would henceforth celebrate the date as marking the enemy's surrender, making skilful use of photographs that showed the American negotiators in weary or exasperated moments.

Now more dependent on his patrons than ever, the dictator took pains to sound internationalist notes in high-profile speeches, even asserting in December 1955 that "to love the USSR is to love Korea."[9] Domestic propaganda, however, dwelt increasingly on the virtues of Koreanness.[10] The translation of foreign works was reduced, and the performance of Soviet plays forbidden altogether.[11] An East German diplomat reported home that all successes were "portrayed as accomplishments of the Korean workers 'without foreign' assistance."[12] He also noted that the party's educational activities were "not oriented toward studying the works of Marxism-Leninism."[13] Instead the purity of the Korean bloodline was stressed. Women who married Eastern European aid workers were accused of "betraying the race".[14] Anyone perceived to have emotional ties to the outside world became suspect. In 1956 Kim purged his party of its Yenan and Soviet-Korean factions, replacing these old communists with comrades-in-arms from his guerilla days.[15]

Meanwhile the regime was pushing through a collectivization of agriculture that went too far even for Moscow's liking. In 1958 the DPRK began emulating China's Great Leap Forward campaign of radical industrialization with its own Ch'ŏllima or Thousand-League Horse Movement, the symbol of which was a Pegasus-style winged horse.[†] Christians were rounded up and sent to prison camps. Such policies, executed at a time when Eastern Europe was "thawing," conveyed to the West the misleading image of a hard-line Stalinist state. In fact they were perfectly compatible not only with North Korean nationalism, which perceives the child race as innately collectivist, but also with Kim Il Sung's insatiable desire to maximize internal security. Whether the Soviet model would improve the nation's

[†] North Korean historians later backdated the start of this movement to 1956 to make it seem less like a copy of its Chinese counterpart. Alas, even conservative South Korean researchers now uncritically accept 1956 as the year the movement began.

standard of living was never the issue; on the contrary, Kim appears to have been wary of feeding his people too well. In a meeting with East Germany's Erich Honecker in 1977 he said that "'the higher the standard of living climbs, the more ideologically lazy and the more careless the activity' of the people is," a statement that, as Berndt Schäfer has remarked, "no East German leader could have gotten away with making."[16] Balazs Szalontai notes that Kim Il Sung "consistently preferred economic 'corrections' that did not loosen the regime's control over society to those which did."[17]

The regime had other reasons for imitating Soviet models. It needed to distinguish itself from a far more populous Korean state which would otherwise have enjoyed a superior claim to legitimacy, and to ensure the continued inflow of economic, diplomatic and military support from abroad. East European diplomats had, however, already begun reporting home about the xenophobia in Pyongyang. Some were cursed and pelted with rocks by children on the street. Koreans who had married Europeans were pressured to divorce or banished from the capital. (Internally the East German embassy compared these practices to Nazi Germany.)[18] One Soviet wife of a Korean citizen was beaten unconscious by provincial police when she attempted to travel to Pyongyang.[19] In 1965, the Cuban ambassador to the DPRK, a black man, was squiring his wife and some Cuban doctors around the city when locals surrounded their car, pounding it and shouting racial epithets.[20] Police called to the scene had to beat the mob back with truncheons. "The level of training of the masses is extremely low," a high-ranking official later told the shaken diplomat. "They cannot

Nikita Khrushchev and Kim Il Sung

distinguish between friends and foes."[21] This was precisely the mindset that the regime sought to instil.

FROM THE CULTURAL REVOLUTION
TO KIM IL SUNG'S DEATH, 1966-1994

Relations between Beijing and Pyongyang worsened in 1966 when China's leader launched the Cultural Revolution. Kim evidently worried that Mao fever might infect his own people, which in turn might encourage Beijing to attempt a coup or an invasion. This was no mere paranoia; Chinese troops did indeed make a few provocative incursions across the North Korean border.[1] Kim's first response was to tighten internal security even further. After a census in 1966, DPRK citizens were divided according to their family background or *sŏngbun* into a "core" class of high-ranking cadres and their families, a "wavering" class of average citizens, and a "hostile" class made up of former landowners and other potential subversives. People of all *sŏngbun* were organized into an exhausting regimen of social activities and study sessions, the latter devoted more to the fantasy biography of Kim than to his writings.

Those who ran afoul of the state faced punishment ranging from the denial of food rations to imprisonment, but the party did not build up a massive police presence, nor did the average citizen live in terror of arrest. Like the colonial government before it, the regime knew how to exploit the Korean people's traditional tendency to conform. The personality cult also played a vital role in garnering support for the regime.[2] With the young Kim Jong Il at its helm, the propaganda apparatus made sure that the cult kept pace with its Chinese counterpart. Mao's renown as a poet, for example, inspired the DPRK's cultural apparatus to "revive" revolutionary plays, hitherto unmentioned, which Kim Il Sung had allegedly written during his youth.[3] It was also "remembered" that in the 1930s the General had taken his partisans on an Arduous March every bit as heroic as Mao's Long March.[4] And if Mao had routed the Japanese without foreign help, then by golly, so had Kim. This last claim necessitated the withdrawal of countless reference works and school books that had paid fawning tribute to the Soviet Red Army.[†]

[†] A North Korean refugee, the son of a poet, told me how plain-clothed police came to the family apartment in Pyongyang at this time to search for such books.

Many in the West wrongly assume, as George Orwell did, that a regime cannot reinvent history without resorting to brainwashing and intimidation. One need only look at the South Koreans, who celebrate their liberation from Japan every year with nary a mention of their liberators, to see how easily nationalist mythmaking goes down even in open societies. But Korean nationalists do not seriously believe that they were never aided by foreigners. Rather, they think that because that aid was motivated by self-interest, it is not historically *meaningful*, nor does it warrant grateful acknowledgment.

Mao's reputation as a thinker posed a greater problem to Kim, who had never even led the discourse of his own party.[5] Scouring his speeches for glimmers of original thought, the executors of the personality cult focused on his conveniently vague use of the Marxist term "subject," or *juche* (chu'che) in Korean. In a speech in December 1955, Kim had reminded

propagandists that the "subject"—the agent, in other words—
of ideological work was the Korean revolution; instead of
merely aping Soviet forms the party needed to establish the
proper "subject" in its propaganda work. This sort of toothless
nationalism or "domesticism" had been *de rigueur* throughout
the East Bloc in the 1950s, for which reason the speech had
aroused no special attention either in Pyongyang or Moscow.
But North Korea watchers in the West, unaware of the greater
communist context, or the standard Marxist use of the word
juche, had been quick to misinterpret the speech as a bold,
epochal declaration of Korean nationalism. (They still make
the same mistake; Kim's line "to love the USSR is to love Korea"
is invariably overlooked.[6]) Their impressed response appears
to have encouraged the North Koreans to begin touting "the
subject idea" in the latter 1960s as Kim Il Sung's original con-
tribution to Marxist thought.

Kim saw no urgent need to create an actual ideology to
back up the cant, but one of his advisors, a self-styled philoso-
pher named Hwang Chang-yŏp, finally persuaded the leader
to entrust him with this task.[7] Hwang had his work cut out for
him because there was nothing in Kim's talk of self-reliance,
or of adapting Marxism-Leninism to national conditions, that
Mao had not only said more eloquently, but had done a much
better job of putting into practice as well. Hwang also had to
be careful not to make the new ideology clear or appealing
enough to distract the domestic masses from the *de facto* ideology of race-based nationalism (which of course could not
be conveyed to the outside world). He had to come up with
something innocuous, impenetrable, yet imposing, and in the
end he did just that.

Hwang's so-called Juche Thought—credited of course to Kim—revealed itself in September 1972, in the form of "an answer to questions from Japanese journalists," as a stodgy jumble of banalities. A representative excerpt from the seminal text:

> Establishing the subject/*juche* means approaching revolution and construction with the attitude of a master. Because the masses are the master of revolution and construction, they must assume a master's attitude in regard to revolution and construction. A master's attitude is expressed in an independent position and a creative position. Revolution and construction are endeavours for the sake of the masses, and endeavours that the masses themselves must carry out. Therefore, in reshaping nature and society an independent position and a creative position are called for.[8]

Only when talking of Juche Thought does the regime express itself in this peculiar style, which is far too repetitive and dull not to be so by design. It recalls a college student trying both to stretch a term paper to a respectable length and to discourage anyone from reading it through. Far more concise and stirring language is used to espouse the true ruling ideology of paranoid nationalism. Though Juche Thought is enshrined in the constitution as one of the country's guiding principles, the regime has never shown any indication of subscribing to its universal-humanist bromides: "man is the master of all things," "people are born with creativity and autonomy," etc. I do not mean to imply that if an ideology is not lived up to, it is *ipso facto* a sham. (Judged by that standard, no ideology will 'scape whipping.) But Juche is not even professed in earnest, and no wonder; its central notion of the masses' mastery of their fate runs counter to the sacrosanct notion of a uniquely vulnerable child race in the Leader's protective care. Koreans must thank him, after all, even for what they earn by their own labor.

The pseudo-doctrine of Juche continues to serve its purpose all the same. It enables the regime to lionize Kim Il Sung as a great thinker, provides an impressive label for whatever policies it considers expedient, and prevents dissidents from judging policy on the government's own ostensible terms. Just as importantly, it decoys outsiders away from the true dominant ideology. Instead of an implacably xenophobic, race-based worldview derived largely from fascist Japanese myth, the world sees a reassuringly dull state-nationalism conceived by post-colonial Koreans, rooted in humanist principles, and evincing an understandable if unfortunate preoccupation with autonomy and self-reliance.

The Juche Tower

But how could foreign scholars read the English-language versions of the official Juche discourse without realizing how empty it is? One answer is that by the time those texts started appearing in the 1970s, North Korea's allegiance to the mysterious doctrine was already accepted overseas as fact. Another answer is that the very incoherence, dullness and evasiveness of Juche convey to the postmodern Western reader an impressive difficulty. Now *this*, he thinks, is what an ideology should look like, as opposed to the race-based nationalism espoused in the DPRK's schoolbooks, films and

paintings, which is too crude and direct to be taken seriously. Even scholars aware of the triteness of the Juche discourse
assume there has to be more to it than meets the eye. The historian Bruce Cumings, in apologetic desperation, concludes
that it is "inaccessible to the non-Korean."[9] As if North Koreans were not as baffled by it as everyone else! The regime's
decision not to publish a comprehensive Juche treatise under
Kim Il Sung's name turns out to have been a stroke of genius.
Whatever one reads, one is always left thinking the profound
stuff must be somewhere else.

The perceived need to pay tribute to the USSR had long
kept the Kim cult within certain boundaries, but in 1972, the
year the leader turned sixty, it surpassed even the Mao cult in
extravagance. Erecting an enormous bronze likeness of him
in Pyongyang's main square, the regime instructed natives
and foreign visitors alike to lay wreaths at its base. An arch of
triumph, far larger than its Parisian model, went up to com-
memorate the leader's anti-Japanese struggle.

Ever since this efflorescence of the personality cult, outside analysts have confidently claimed that the DPRK is in
effect a Confucian family writ large, with Kim Il Sung as the
father, the Workers' Party as the mother, and the people as
the children.[10] A nice and neat theory, to be sure, but only the
latter half of it holds up. In fact Kim Il Sung was increasingly
acclaimed by the androgynous title of Parent Leader (ŏbŏi
suryŏng), and like Hirohito was more a mother figure than a
patriarch. By its own admission, the Workers' Party calls itself
the Mother Party not because it complements but because it
emulates both Kims' style of leadership.[11] This prevalence of
maternal authority figures is hard if not impossible to recon-

The statue of Kim Il Sung on
Pyongyang's Mansu Hill

cile with Confucianism, which dictates that a mother must obey even her own sons.

Most North Korean refugees remember the 1970s as a happy time. Food, energy and clothing were in far more plentiful supply than they are today, Pyongyang's proud rhetoric not having stopped it from squeezing even Bulgaria and Cuba for economic aid. As the DPRK saw things, it had shown its moral superiority by rejecting, at no small cost to its standard of living, all concessions to capitalism. It was only right and proper that inferior races should pay tribute by sharing some of their ill-gotten gains. Though much of the aid was provided in terms of loans, the DPRK made little effort to repay them.

In 1982 Kim Jong Il joined the Supreme People's Assembly, assumed the title of Dear Leader, and became the object of his own extravagant personality cult.[†] Much was made of his birth on sacred Mount Paektu (though he had really been born in the USSR), his loving care for his father, and his alleged expertise in cultural matters, especially film-making. While foreigners regarded the planned succession as additional evidence of Confucian tendencies, Kim Jong Il emerged as an even more maternal figure than his father had been. He was, as one novelist put it, "More of a mother than all the mothers in the world."[12]

Where the pseudo-doctrine of Juche Thought made much of the need for self-reliance, the DPRK's economic policy reflected a commitment to isolation instead, which is something very different. It is perhaps helpful to draw an analogy to *hikikomori*, young Japanese men who refuse to venture out of their bedrooms, instead demanding that parents leave meal trays outside their door. They feel they can preserve

[†] Dear Ruler might be a more accurate translation, because the Korean word chidoja—or yŏngdoja, as is now more common—is different from the word suryŏng used in Kim Il Sung's title of Parent Leader.

their independence better by relying on the outside world than by working with it.[13] Similarly, Kim Il Sung appears to have believed that the best way of maximizing his country's isolation and security was not to strengthen the economy—a goal that would have required integration into the socialist trading community and other horrors—but rather to rely indefinitely on aid. This is not to deny that North Korea has always done many things for itself. One cannot depend *completely* on outsiders without forfeiting one's isolation, or at least one's privacy. (The *hikikomori* cleans his own room.) When a form of aid serves isolation, the North Koreans take it indefinitely, and when it does not, they do without; a concern for self-reliance *per se* does not enter into things. Especially telling, in this regard, is Pyongyang's history of squandering currency reserves on luxury imports.[14]

The DPRK was thus caught flat-footed in 1987 when the USSR began sharply reducing its aid to the country. Two years later the East German leader Erich Honecker was forced out of office and into exile, much to Kim Il Sung's consternation. German unification was quick to follow. Meanwhile Moscow began demanding that the DPRK pay world market prices for Soviet goods.[15] Imports dropped accordingly.[16] With the food supply worsening throughout the early 1990s, the party launched the slogan "Let's Eat Two Meals a Day" and stepped up the glorification of self-sacrificing "hidden heroes" in remote farms and factories.[17]

On July 8, 1994, the eighty-two year old Parent Leader passed away—from overwork, news announcers wailed—and the DPRK immediately contracted, to borrow a line from *Hamlet*, in one brow of woe. Orgies of weeping took place in city and town squares across the country. Some refugees who were children at the time remember desperately trying to force tears, but most adults appear to have been genuinely grief-stricken—or at least afraid of a future without the only leader they had ever known. It was perhaps fortunate for the regime that Kim died when he did. Had he lived a few years longer, the economic collapse would have done irrevocable damage to his reputation. As it was, the famine of 1995-1997 appeared to offer retroactive proof that the Parent Leader had indeed been single-handedly feeding and clothing his people up to his death.

THE ARDUOUS MARCH, 1994-1998

By the time Kim Il Sung died, it was already taken for granted, both inside and outside the DPRK, that his son would take over. Kim Jong Il had assumed command of the country's armed forces in 1991, and his fiftieth birthday in 1992 had occasioned a massive celebration, complete with the bizarre (and utterly un-Confucian) spectacle of the Parent Leader penning a panegyric to his own son.[1] The threat to withdraw the DPRK from the Non-Proliferation Treaty in 1992, the placing of the country on a war footing in 1993: these and related measures, which were said to have brought Jimmy Carter to Pyongyang in June 1994 to negotiate the Yankee surrender, were largely credited to Kim Jong Il's genius and resolve.[2] The nuclear crisis thus endowed the heir to the throne with his own myth of national rescue, and not a moment too soon.

The Dear Leader took over in July 1994 without formally replacing his late father; to this day Kim Il Sung remains the

"Eternal President" of the country. Meanwhile food production was in a free fall, not least because of the disruptions caused by mourning ceremonies. By the end of 1994 the ration system had all but ceased functioning outside Pyongyang. At first the regime tried to brazen out the crisis by trumpeting the record harvest sown by the Parent Leader in his last months.[3] It soon realized, however, that to continue in such a vein would be to risk forfeiting its credibility altogether. Public expectations for the new leader had to be sharply reduced before the food shortage worsened into famine. After lying low for a few months, a somber Kim Jong Il appeared in 1995 at the head of a "military first" government compelled (or so the media claimed) to devote all its time and energy to national defense.

Ironically enough, relations between Washington and Pyongyang had never been better: the Agreed Framework had been signed in October 1994, President Clinton had sent Kim a groveling letter promising full compliance, and energy aid was already flowing in. Kim thus found himself in the awkward position of having to nurture Washington's hope for better relations while at the same time whipping up anti-Americanism at home. Aware that the language barrier forced most outside observers to focus on the official news agency's English-language service, Kim had it tone down its invective and refrain from vilifying the US president by name. Meanwhile, in domestic propaganda, the Agreed Framework was crowed over as an abject Yankee surrender. A glorious battle had been won, but not the war; for the "jackals" could never change their inherently rapacious nature. Hence the need for the Dear Leader to spend most of his time visiting military bases, from the Yalu River in the north to the DMZ in the south. Much as it pained him, the provinces would have to take self-reliance to the next level and begin feeding themselves. Official media lamented the hardship suffered by Kim on his tireless tour. His famed diet of "whatever the troops are eating" was routinely invoked to shame everyone into working harder.

But although the Dear Leader remained popular, the economy was collapsing, and taking internal security down with it. Outside Pyongyang, social discipline had already broken down. Many citizens stayed away from work for weeks on end, re-appearing only to plunder their factories. This decline in the authority of the workplace was all the more significant because for the average citizen it had been the center of political life as well.[4] Soldiers roamed the countryside in search of food, robbing civilians and sometimes engaging in armed clashes with the police. Corpses lay on the steps of train stations. Refugees have provided credible testimony of widespread cannibalism.[5] Foreign experts now estimate that about a million people—roughly 5 percent of the population—died from hunger-related causes during the worst period of the famine, from 1995 to 1997.[6]

By the late 1990s the DPRK's northern border was very loosely or corruptly policed, and tens of thousands of citizens from the northeast crossed the Tumen River into China. Though there were far fewer migrants than might have been expected, and those who left the country did so only to return with smuggled goods, the influx of South Korean videos and reports of Chinese prosperity greatly eroded the information cordon that had once sealed the DPRK off from the outside world.

To the world's surprise, this development did not significantly undermine support for the regime. Refugees claim that people were just too hungry to think of politics. An equally obvious explanation is that people do not easily toss aside a worldview dinned into them since childhood. But also important is the *nature* of that worldview. By the mid-1990s the North Koreans had ceased paying even lip service to Marxism-Leninism.[7] Socialism or "our style of socialism" had come to mean only "how we do things," capitalism a catchword for "how Yankees enslave the southern brethren."[8] It was because the regime no longer derived its legitimacy from a commitment to improve material conditions that it did not have to deny there was an economic crisis, something the Soviet and Chinese parties had destroyed their own credibility by doing.

Needless to say, the regime neither acknowledged the full extent of the food shortage—the word famine was never used—nor accepted any responsibility for it. Instead one spoke of economic "difficulties" while blaming them on bad weather, Yankee sanctions and lazy mid-level bureaucrats. All this, it must be noted, was at least partially true. If anything, the famine may have strengthened support for the regime by renewing the sense of ethnic victimhood from which the official worldview derived its passion. Many migrants remember a widespread yearning for war with America during the famine.[9]

THE SUNSHINE YEARS, 1998-2008

By 1998 the worst of the food shortage was over, and the official media had begun to cheer Kim Jong Il for dashing the Yankees' dreams of regime change. Tasteless though these congratulations may have been, they were well-deserved, for the DPRK had survived a crisis far worse than the mere malaise that had seen off the communist bloc a decade earlier. In a new flurry of confidence the regime announced the forward-looking slogan "A Great Country, Strong and Prosperous" (kangsŏng taeguk), and agreed to a meeting between Kim Jong Il and the South Korean president Kim Dae Jung, the advocate of a new "Sunshine Policy" of reconciliation with the North. The summit took place in June 2000 in Pyongyang and ended in the so-called June 15 Declaration, in which both sides pledged to work peacefully "among ourselves" towards the goal of unification. There ensued massive infusions of unconditional aid from Seoul, much of it in the form of cash.

For all its help in financing his military and nuclear program, the Sunshine Policy put Kim Jong Il in a difficult position. He could hardly admit that the ROK wanted friendlier relations, because this would mean it was no Yankee puppet after all. Neither could he endanger the flow of aid by continuing to vilify his counterpart in Seoul as if nothing had happened. So it was that the official news agency ceased its attacks on the South Korean government, and less prominent propaganda outlets picked up the slack. The latter asserted that Kim Dae Jung had come to Pyongyang in 2000 to make the North renounce socialism, only to be dazed by the Dear

† A former secret police operative from the harbor city of Namp'o told me that to spread this distorted view of the summit she and other colleagues were made to visit towns and villages posing as well-connected travelers from Pyongyang.

Leader's genius into accepting his demands for inter-Korean cooperation.† The ensuing years saw the regime devote ever more energy to demonizing the Republican administration in Washington. In 2002, President George W. Bush's reference to North Korea as part of an "axis of evil" was met with aggrieved posturing by the KCNA (which since its founding in 1948 had vigorously applied the word "evil" to the United States). Propaganda contradicted itself: On the one hand the Americans' allegations of a nuclear weapons program were condemned as far-fetched lies, while on the other it was truculently implied that they were true. "Under the pretext of a so-called 'nuclear problem' the US is making its military threats against our republic ever more explicit," wrote a KCNA scribe in May 2003, weeks after North Korea withdrew from the Nuclear Non-Proliferation Treaty. "The only way to guard the nation's peace…under these circumstances, which cause such deep concern to the entire Korean people, is to have a strong deterrent against war. We have already prepared such a military deterrent."[1]

By the summer of 2003 the DPRK had agreed to take part in nuclear negotiations with the US, China, Japan, Russia and South Korea. While the regime's diplomats expressed hope for better relations, domestic propaganda stridently insisted that the Yankees were inherently evil and would never change. In August, with the first round of the six-party talks about to convene in Beijing, *Jackals* (1951), the canonical tale of murderous Christian missionaries, re-appeared simultaneously in three monthly magazines, complete with drawings of sunken-eyed, hook-nosed Yankees.[2]

The DPRK's recovery from the famine years did not mean a full restoration of the internal security of old. Many in the northern provinces continued tuning in to Chinese TV on their smuggled sets, and communicating with migrants by smuggled cell phones. Some near the DMZ had even taken to watching television broadcasts from Seoul. Despite periodic crackdowns by the authorities, South Korean videos and DVD's did a roaring trade in rural markets.

As a result, the South's prosperity quickly became common knowledge inside the DPRK. Realizing that it would do no good to deny it, the propaganda apparatus in 2000 began openly admitting that South Koreans enjoy a higher standard of living. This prosperity was rather ingeniously attributed to the Dear Leader's "military-first" policy, which had allegedly kept the Yankees from unleashing another ruinous war on the peninsula. At the same time, of course, it was claimed that despite their wealth, the southern brethren yearned to rout their oppressors and rush to the Dear Leader's embrace.

This line was not as preposterous as all that. Koreans in both republics generally agree that they are a uniquely homogenous, i.e. pure-blooded people whose innate goodness has made them perennial victims of foreign powers. While the DPRK expresses itself more stridently on such matters, there has never been as sharp an ideological divide as the one that separated West and East Germany. The dictators that ruled the ROK until the late 1980s thus had to keep strenuously downplaying the rival state's Koreanness, referring to it as "the northern monster," a Soviet satellite of strange "reds"; these were depicted primarily in animated cartoons. (Middle-aged South Koreans recall with a chuckle how in their childhood they had believed the "reds" were literally red!) The rise of public sympathy for the DPRK in the late 1990s was caused not by pro-Pyongyang propaganda but by the mere disappearance of the anti-Pyongyang kind: "As soon as we saw that they are Korean too, we stopped hating them," is a typically naive account of the change. In the ROK's southwestern provinces, a hotbed of left-wing sentiment and anti-Americanism, one encounters widespread sympathy even for the North Korean dictator himself.

Although South Koreans are glad that they compromised their nationalist principles for wealth and modernity, many of them feel a nagging sense of moral inferiority to their more orthodox brethren. They may disapprove of the North's actions, but rarely with indignation, often blaming America or Japan for having provoked them. Eager to assuage their guilt about not wanting re-unification, they prefer to see in the DPRK's lack of democracy and human rights only a benign difference in stages of development.

The Kim Dae Jung and Roh Moo Hyun administrations that ruled the country from 1998 to 2008 heightened these tendencies by encouraging an anti-American line in education and urging the media to "finlandize" their coverage of the DPRK. As a result, a North Korean surreptitiously watching TV broadcasts from Seoul would have seen little in these years that *directly* contradicted the myth of a rich-but-shamefaced South chafing under the Yankee yoke. Instead he would have heard news announcers referring respectfully to Kim Jong Il as the "National Defense Council Chairman," a title that implicitly acknowledged the legitimacy of both the North Korean state and its nuclear program. He would have seen numerous anti-American demonstrations, attended by tens of thousands of South Koreans of all ages and economic classes. He would have learned of the opinion polls according to which the US is the country most widely perceived as South Korea's main enemy. He might even have seen romantic comedies in which a virginal girl from the North appears as the better, purer Korean.

None of this, however, discouraged the DPRK's youth from trying to follow the Yankee colony's music, slang and fashions. The regime responded by condemning the influx of heterodox culture and information as a CIA plot to destabilize the republic. A lecture written in spring 2005 for party-internal use (and later smuggled out of the DPRK) quotes Kim Jong Il as saying, "Through all manner of falsehoods and trickery, the imperialists and reactionaries are paralyzing the healthy thinking of the masses while spreading among them bourgeois-reactionary ideas and rotten bourgeois customs."[3] These included living in a lazy, corrupt or decadent fashion, wearing long hair and clothes with "politically problematic words or pictures on them," and otherwise copying other countries' ways.[4]

> What will happen if we succumb to and fail to block these customs of living that the bastards are disseminating? In a word, we become…incapable of adhering to socialism. Most importantly, we become unable to defend to our death the leadership of the revolution.[5]

But while outside cultural influences were much in evidence, even in Pyongyang itself, no credible visitor to the DPRK registered significant signs of political dissent. One aid worker said that the only criticism he had heard in weeks touring the country in 2005 came from a drunken man who said, "People would prefer a better life."† Nor was there evidence to support claims that a Christian multitude was secretly worshipping there.[6] The closest thing to a popular non-secular activity appeared to be the consultation of shamans and fortune-tellers for business advice.[7] There were, for that matter, no reliable indications that North Koreans engaged in any illegal forms of associational life that were not aimed at making money. Nor did they consider their entrepreneurial activities to be at odds with the official ideology. "Making money is patriotic" was said to be a popular if informal slogan.[8] In short, the spread of capitalism did not appear to be eroding support for the regime.

THE DPRK IN CRISIS, 2008-

Though never going so far as to praise either of the left-wing presidents to occupy the Blue House in Seoul, the North had for most of the decade concentrated its invective on the "warmongers" and "Yankee lackeys" in South Korea's conservative opposition. As the presidential election campaign got underway in the rival state in 2007, the KCNA zeroed in on the "traitor" Lee Myung Bak, who was then campaigning on pledges to strengthen the alliance with the USA and cease unconditional aid to the North. When Kim Jong Il agreed to a second North-South summit in October 2007, many South Korean commentators expected him to offer a spectacular concession to the outgoing President Roh, thus countering Lee's criticism of the Sunshine Policy and boosting chances for the pro-Pyongyang candidate.

But the deterioration of the information cordon since the first summit in 2000 had changed things. Kim Jong Il could no longer hope to pull off the feat of posing to the South as a jovial peace-maker while posing to the North as the condescending host to a tributary delegation. What the one half of the peninsula would hear and see of the summit, the other was likely to hear and see as well. The General had no choice but to put his domestic image first. At their first meeting, which took place outdoors, he stood stock-still and poker-faced as the broadly smiling Roh approached to shake his hand. The South Korean delegation claimed that Kim warmed up behind closed doors the next day, but word soon spread that he had mocked his counterpart for being unable to decide on his own whether to stay a few days longer. If billions of dollars in unconditional aid had effected an improvement in inter-Korean relations since 2000, there was no sign of it. The summit ended in another declaration averring both sides' determination to work towards unification, but the damage had been done. The South Korean electorate's disaffection with the Sunshine Policy played an important role in helping the conservative candidate win in November.

Had the Kim regime been misled by the sheer vociferousness and visibility of South Korea's anti-American left into doubting pollsters' predictions of a Lee victory? Perhaps. The propaganda apparatus certainly appeared to have been caught off guard by the election results when South Korean TV announced them in November 2007. What to say to the North Korean public? With so many citizens now accessing outside sources of information, none of which had criticized the vote-counting process, it was not feasible to claim that Lee had stolen the election. But neither could the truth be conceded that the southern brethren had chosen the pro-Yankee candidate; this would mean either that the Korean race was not so pure after all, or, even more unthinkably, that there was something in the Dear Leader that had alienated them.

For several weeks the official media simply said nothing about Lee's triumph. (The apposite Korean phrase: *muksal*, to kill with silence.) Finally, in early 2008, it began asserting that the "traitor" had hoodwinked the electorate by keeping his true political intentions secret. For decades so surefooted in its strategy, the propaganda apparatus was now reduced to hoping the masses would not remember its criticism of Lee's campaign platform! But luck was on Kim Jong Il's side. Hardly had the new president taken office than the South Korean public lashed itself into another of its xenophobic frenzies. This time the occasion was the administration's intention to open the beef market to American imports. As rumors spread of a unique Korean susceptibility to mad cow disease, massive crowds took to the streets of Seoul denouncing Lee as a dictator and traitor, and accusing the Yankees of saving their most diseased meat for the peninsula. Many of the demonstrators interviewed by reporters said they felt cruelly deceived by a man they had just voted into power. The Kim regime could not have asked for a more timely and dramatic confirmation of its propaganda; it gloated over the crisis for months while exhorting the southern brethren to rise up and sweep the puppet state from power.

But by summer 2008 the beef crisis had passed. Realizing that Lee was in the Blue House to stay, the Kim regime turned a critical eye to the two North-South cooperation projects upon which it had embarked during the Sunshine Policy era. Clearly, the economic benefits to be derived from the Mount Kumgang tourist resort and the Kaesong Industrial Zone (both just north of the DMZ) were not worth the political dangers of being seen to be cooperating, even indirectly, with the "traitor" in Seoul. The party was in any case growing increasingly concerned about the intermingling between local staff and Hyundai employees at these sites. When a KPA soldier in July 2008 shot and killed a South Korean tourist who had strayed into a restricted area at Mount Kumgang, the Kim regime offered no apology. President Lee responded by suspending all trips to the resort.

On September 8, 2008, Kim Jong Il failed to appear in public at a military parade celebrating North Korea's sixtieth anniversary, a milestone to which the official media had been building up for months. The world press soon began receiving information that Kim had suffered a stroke in August. Speculation about his health intensified throughout the autumn, punctuated by rumors that he had already died, until there finally appeared a few topical and authentic-looking pictures from his endless "on-the-spot guidance" tour. The pudgy, expansively gesticulating General of old had given way to a thin, slack-faced man with one gloved hand hooked awkwardly in the pocket of his jacket. The propaganda apparatus had evidently concluded that offering visual evidence of a stroke was better than letting the world run riot with rumors of an even more subversive nature, but the decision cannot have been an easy one. (Physical infirmity always carries a greater stigma in states that espouse a race theory; the goiter on Kim Il Sung's neck had had to be kept

a strict secret.) Such were the challenges of maintaining a personality cult in the absence of an information cordon.

The photographs did nothing to stop outside journalists from wondering who was next in line for the succession. It was soon learned that young North Koreans had been taught to sing a song glorifying a certain General Kim, whose vigorous stride (so the lyric) was making the very rivers and mountains rejoice. That this General was not the current leader, whose name is invariably invoked in its full three syllables, was clear enough, ergo the poem's subject had to be the successor to the throne. But the lyric offered no further clues as to which of Kim Jong Il's sons by his various wives was meant. Various names were bruited about in South Korea and elsewhere over the next few weeks, with expert consensus finally settling on Kim Jong Un, the second son of the Dear Leader's third wife. Meanwhile the North Korean media stuck to its longstanding policy of acting as if the Dear Leader had no wife or offspring at all.

The regime spent the spring of 2009 launching missiles from sites on the east coast and urging the masses, under the slogan of a "150 Day Battle," to farm and produce more, the better to strengthen the country against the Yankee enemy. The deliberate ratcheting up of tension did not discourage former US president Bill Clinton from arriving in Pyongyang in August 2009 to secure the release of two American journalists who had been arrested in March for illegally entering the country. Kim Jong Il, it was soon learned, had agreed in advance to look favorably on the request in return for his erstwhile foe's spectacular pilgrimage. Fittingly enough, the party newspaper carried photographs of Kim and Clinton sitting before an enormous painting of waves crashing on rocks, a standard symbol of the country's resolve to stand up to a hostile outside world.

Hardly had the "150 Day Battle" ended amid great fanfare in September than a "100 Day Battle" was embarked upon. Rumor had it that speakers at party lectures and workplaces assemblies were crediting these glorious enthusiasm campaigns to Kim Jong Il's young heir. The national broadcast and print media, however, had still not mentioned him; evidently the goal was to keep the outside world in the dark for as long as possible. At last, in September 2009, a Taiwanese tourist photographed a wall poster that congratulated the masses on having not only the Dear General to take care of them, but the "young General" too. The latter's full name was written in the blood-red ink reserved for names in the Kim Il Sung line: Kim Jong Ŭn. As of the time of this writing, it was not yet certain whether he and the Kim Jong Un of outside news reports were one and the same, but the likelihood appeared very high. It seemed no less probable that the succession would be formally announced by or during 2012, the hundredth anniversary of Kim Il Sung's birth and the year in which the DPRK was to attain to the status of "a strong and prosperous country."

Whatever kind of country the successor stands to inherit, it will not be a communist one. The DPRK's revised constitution, ratified in April 2009 and made known to the world in the fall, forbore even to pay lip service to that term, instead invoking "military-first" socialism as the country's guiding principle. Short of reviving the kamikaze slogans of the Pacific War—though of course it has done that too—the regime can hardly make its ideological affinity to the first "national defense" state on Korean soil any clearer. Whether the world will ever stop regarding the DPRK as "the last bastion of Stalinism" is another matter.

PART II

Understanding North Korea Through Its Myths

CHAPTER TWO
MOTHER KOREA AND HER CHILDREN

In May 2006 North and South Korean generals met to discuss a re-alignment of the maritime border between the two states. In preliminary small talk the South's delegation leader mentioned that farmers in his half of the peninsula had taken to marrying women from other countries. His counterpart made no effort to hide his displeasure. "Our nation has always considered its pure lineage to be of great importance," he said. "I am concerned that our singularity will disappear." The

South Korean, dismissing such marriages as a mere "drop of ink in the Han River," responded that the mainstream would suffice to preserve the nation's identity. More concerned with racial purity than cultural identity, the DPRK general replied, "Since ancient times our land has been one of abundant natural beauty. Not even one drop of ink must be allowed."[1]

Although foreign journalists took amused note of this exchange, it did not discourage them from referring to the DPRK as a "hard-line communist" state.[2] They seem to have assumed that the North Korean officer was speaking off the record. In fact his remarks were fully in line with the official ideology. Only weeks earlier, the party daily had condemned the South Korean government for welcoming an American star football player of half-Korean parentage and for tolerating miscegenation:

> Mono-ethnicity [tanilsŏng] is something that our nation and no other on earth can pride itself on...There is no suppressing the nation's shame and anger at the talk of "a multi-ethnic, multi-racial society"...which would dilute even the bloodline of our people.[3]

Even the general's seemingly irrelevant remark about Korea's natural beauty was orthodox. One of the many correspondences between the North Korean worldview and European fascist thought is the notion of a mystical unity between the nation and its territory. (German *Völkisch* theorists believed the Jews, being originally of the desert, were naturally shallow and dry.)[4] The regime never tires of conveying the message, not least through the monumental landscape paintings before which the leader receives foreign dignitaries, that the motherland's physical attributes—from the loftiness of its peaks to the purity of its mountain lakes—reflect the virtues of the race itself.

An especially common motif is the deep forest, which psychologists regard as a universal archetype of the instincts. Informed as they are by our traditional mistrust of spontaneity, our fairy-tales and legends tend to depict the forest as a menacing place of witches and wolves. The North Koreans, with their celebration of pure racial instincts, treat it as a safe and womb-like place that affords them an insurmountable advantage over the enemy. Another popular image, especially since the collapse of the national economy in the early 1990s, is that of giant waves hurling themselves against the motherland's rocky coast.

Use of the word "motherland" in this context may surprise Western readers who, proceeding from the popular fallacy of a Confucian-cum-Stalinist state, tend to expect North Koreans to think in terms of a fatherland instead. That is indeed the word more often used in the KCNA's English-language service.[5] But when propaganda for domestic consumption—or what for convenience's sake I call the Text—compares the country to one of the two parents, it is always to a mother: the most common term is literally "mother homeland."[6] Kim Jong Il himself is quoted as saying, "The homeland is everyone's mother...[from whose] bosom all true life and happiness springs."[7]

A mythologized version of Mother Korea's history is at the heart of the Text. It can be summarized as follows.

Thousands of years ago, on a beautiful peninsula in the center of East Asia, there emerged one of mankind's first distinct races, the Korean race. While still evolving from Early Korean to Modern Korean Man the Koreans settled the whole peninsula and much of northeast Asia. All they lacked was a strong leader. At last, in the third millennium BE, a great emperor named Tan'gun united Koreans into a state named Chosŏn, taking Pyongyang as his capital. Koreans were thus the first Asians to achieve nationhood, a crucial first stage of civilization. Though Old Chosŏn shared the peninsula with other, smaller kingdoms, the Koreans were always one people with the same blood, language, culture and lofty morals. In the year 918 they were united once more. Alas, foreign aggressors, resentful of Korea's autonomy and greedy for its natural riches, refused to leave the peace-loving people alone. Only by repeatedly driving back invading forces—from Chinese tribes to Japanese samurai to American war ships—was the Korean race able to preserve its unique integrity up to the present day.

From the start Koreans were marked by a strong sense of virtue and justice, and their exemplary manners earned the country renown as "The Land of Politeness in the East." No less famous were their clothes, which were as white as the snow-capped peaks of Mount Paektu. Kind-hearted and well featured, Koreans lived in harmonious villages, respecting the people above them and loving those beneath them. Unfortunately the effete ruling classes, having fallen under the sway of Confucianism, Buddhism and other pernicious foreign ideologies, proved no match for the imperialists' schemes, and in 1905 Korea became a Japanese colony. Burning with righteous anger, the masses rose up on March 1, 1919 to demand national independence.

The demonstration was brutally suppressed. Fortunately a great leader had already been born who would guide the nation to its proper place on the world stage.[8]

The regime in Pyongyang is often accused of "brainwashing" its subjects, as if the former secretly believed something very different, and the latter were passive or even unwilling victims of indoctrination. Perhaps this misperception derives from the mistaken belief that the personality cult—which looks much harder to swallow when regarded in isolation—forms the basis of the official worldview. In fact, as we can see from the above summary, the personality cult proceeds from myths about the race and its history that cannot but exert a strong appeal on the North Korean masses. In his classic book *The Denial of Death* (1973), the social anthropologist Ernest Becker concluded that man's fear of death and insignificance makes him look to his country for an "immortality project," a myth that will make him feel "vital to the universe, immortal in some way."[9] The notion of every citizen's sacred mission to reunite the pure race and move it to the center of the world stage does a very good job of filling the North Koreans' need for significance, not least because everyone is given a role to play.

As discussed in the preceding chapter, it was the Japanese who taught the Koreans to see themselves as part of a uniquely pure and virtuous race. All the Kim Il Sung regime did was to expel the Japanese from that race and transpose the familiar Japanese symbols into Korean ones—replacing the divine racial founder Jimmu with the homegrown Tan'gun, Mount Fuji with Mount Paektu, and so on. History books now treat the Tan'gun myth, including the story of his birth on Paektu, as fact. In 1993 the regime claimed to have excavated the great man's tomb near Pyongyang.[10] This is not the place to discuss

In the late 1940s, propaganda began celebrating Mount Paektu, hitherto known merely as Korea's highest peak, as a sacred racial symbol à la Mount Fuji. South Korean veneration of Mount Paektu did not begin until decades later.

whether Tan'gun really existed, or whether Korea's history was as traumatic as all that. As Walker Connor pointed out, "it is seldom *what is* that is of political importance, but what people *think is*."[11] Much the same myths (sans the Kim cult, of course) are widely believed in the southern half of the peninsula too, despite the freedom of speech and information enjoyed there. The main difference is that North Korea regards the country's history as a long foreshadowing to Kim Il Sung, much as Christians see everything before the birth of Jesus as a *Vorgeschichte* or pre-history.

Also unique to the DPRK is the effort to puff up Pyongyang's historical importance at Seoul's expense.[12] The capital is second only to the snow-capped, lake-filled crater of Mount Paektu as the national landmark and geographical symbol of racial purity. The destruction of the original city by American bombs enabled the regime to re-design it from scratch as a grand and enduring work of propaganda in its own right: enormous monuments, most of them constructed in the Soviet-subsidized golden age of the 1970s and 1980s, face each other across wide plazas and boulevards. These include the giant bronze statue of Kim Il Sung, which would dwarf any Mao statue in China; the Arch of Triumph, far larger than its obvious Parisian model; the monument of the winged Ch'ŏllima horse; and, on the other side of the Taedong River, the Juche Tower, complete with a ruby-red electric flame on top that lights up at night; and the monument to the Workers' Party, i.e. gigantic stone renderings of a hoe (for the farmers), a hammer (for industrial workers) and a writing brush (for the white collar workers). Foreigners sneer at the kitsch of these things, cluck about the money spent on their construction, and assume—as is falsely assumed of Nazi buildings—that their imposing size is meant to make people feel insignificant. But propaganda is never a mere waste of money, and its whole point is to make people feel as significant as possible. No doubt North Koreans feel as much pride in these enduring monuments of strength and unity as Americans feel at the sight of the Lincoln Memorial.

White is the dominant color in Pyongyang: white concrete plazas, white or at least blonde-stoned buildings and white statues of virginal maidens in long gowns abound, as could only be possible in a city with none of the heavy industry that Stalin and Mao allowed to develop in urban centers. Pyongyang is often photographed or depicted under snow, a favored symbol of purity in itself.

> The snowstorm rendered Pyongyang—this city steeped in the five-thousand year old, jade-like spirit of the race, imbued with the proudly lonely life-breath of the world's cleanest, most civilized people—free of the slightest blemish. . . covering everything in a thick white veil of purity.[13]

White is made much of throughout the official culture. There is constant reference to the child race's legendary preference for white clothes. In a painting dealing with what the regime calls the Homeland Liberation War (1950-1953) a camou-flaged river-raft and its military cargo are steered by a girl in a dazzling white *chŏgori* or traditional blouse.[14] In an equally improbable painting Kim Il Sung's female partisans wash their whites in a creek, while others hang theirs where they can be seen for miles around. (No men are in sight; in the DPRK, washing is women's work.)[15]

It goes without saying that this propaganda could not be further removed from a Marxist worldview. There is, after all, a great difference between patriotic or state-nationalist com-munism à la Tito's Yugoslavia, and the North Koreans' belief in their innate moral superiority to all other peoples. But for obvious reasons the regime does not advance its race theory explicitly enough to offend its dwindling group of foreign friends. It has little need to be explicit, however, for there is no other worldview inside North Korea against which it must assert itself.[16][†] Occasionally Kim Il Sung will be quoted as having said, for example, "Korea's citizens are homogenous; therefore they have strong brotherly love," or his son quoted as saying that "our people is... the purest and cleanest in the world."[17] But the official race theory is generally propagated more through omission and implication. By stressing that Koreans exhibited "lofty moral attitudes" from the earliest stages of their civilization, and by leaving out the positive mention of formative influences on the national character—Confucianism, Buddhism, Christianity and shamanism are all denounced—the masses are given no choice but to infer that they are born virtuous.[18]

No physical superiority over other races is claimed. Propaganda freely acknowledges, for example, that Americans are much taller.[19] Nor is superior intelligence asserted with any real conviction, though Kim Jong Il has described Koreans as "sensible" and "prudent," and propaganda acclaims the will power they show in the face of adversity.[20] To be uniquely virtuous in an evil world but not uniquely cunning or strong is to be as vulnerable as a child, and indeed, history books convey the image of a perennial child-nation on the world stage, wanting only to be left in peace yet subjected to endless abuse and contamination from outsiders. Films and novels routinely show invaders mistreating Korean children. A standard image of the colonial era is of an exhausted little girl turning a rotary grain mill.[21]

The race's historical vulnerability to attack is ascribed to the absence of a great leader who could turn its purity into

[†]The collapse of the information cordon that once sealed the North off from the "Yankee colony" has changed little in this regard, since the ROK's media has strongly xenophobic tendencies itself. See for example the South Korean newspaper article "Oegugin bŏmjoi kŭpchŭng" (Drastic increase in foreigner crime, Chosun ilbo, October 18, 2007), which is accompanied by an illustration of a Korean girl fleeing in terror from knife-wielding big-noses.

a source of unity and strength. Since the advent of Kim Il Sung, Koreans can and should indulge their pure childlike instincts. For this reason the party poses as a nurturing, protective mother. The *Rodong sinmun* newspaper explained the metaphor in 2003:

> The Great Ruler Comrade Kim Jong Il has remarked, "Building the party into a mother party means that just as a mother deeply loves her children and cares warmly for them, so must the party take responsibility for the fate of the people, looking after them even in the smallest matters, and become a true guide and protector of the masses."[22]

Accordingly, citizens are expected to behave like children. The following is an excerpt from "Mother" (Ŏmŏni), one of the country's best-known poems.

> Ah, Korean Workers' Party
> At whose breast only
> My life begins and ends;
> Be I buried in the ground or strewn to the wind
> I remain your son, and again return to your breast!
> Entrusting my body to your affectionate gaze,
> Your loving outstretched hand,
> I will forever cry out in the voice of a child,
> Mother! I can't live without Mother![23]

It goes without saying that this state-sponsored infantilism exerts a strong psychological appeal. Erich Fromm wrote of how man's fear of emerging from the warm security of the family keeps him "in the prison of the motherly racial-national-religious fixation."[24] No less obvious is the incompatibility of this propaganda with Marxism-Leninism. Believing that "the people is an eternal child," as the French revolutionary Saint-Just famously remarked, Lenin saw the communist party's *raison d'être* in forcing it to grow up.[25] The Soviet party posed as an educating father, as did the dictator who so famously talked of the need to "re-engineer" the human soul. A leading American scholar of Stalinist culture has shown that the so-called spontaneity-consciousness dialectic forms the master plot of socialist realist fiction.[26] Nikolai Ostrovsky's *How the Steel Was Tempered* (Kak zakalyalas' stal', 1936), for example, tells how a party cadre, armed with the teachings of Lenin and Stalin, educates a headstrong youth into a politically conscious "positive hero."

In contrast, the DPRK's propaganda is notably averse to scenes of intellectual discipline. Because Koreans are born pure and selfless, they can and should heed their instincts. Often they are shown breaking out of intellectual constraints in a mad spree of violence against the foreign or land-owning enemy.[27] Cadres are expected to nurture, not teach, and bookworms are negative characters. In short: where Stalinism put the intellect over the instincts, North Korean culture does the opposite. When a sympathetic British documentary about life in the DPRK entitled *A State of Mind* (2004) was shown in Pyongyang, the authorities changed the title to "Maŭm ŭi nara," or *The Country of Heart*.[28]

How do artists depict this spontaneous child race? The men in posters are robust but boyish, with somewhat swarthy complexions, thick eyebrows, square jaws and full lips, the women plump but girlish, with round pale faces and low nose bridges. For all the stylization the faces are recognizably Korean, and although replicating the ideal is more difficult in movies than in posters, most of the country's film stars come close.[29] The men's hair is always short, the women's usually above the shoulders and permed. Little boys' heads are shaven on the sides while young girls sport neat bobs. (To counter the infiltration of South Korean hairstyles, the propaganda apparatus emphasizes the advantages of a very short "military-first" cut.)[30]

The physiognomic ideal admits of little variation. A worker in one painting appears much like a farmer or a soldier in another, while the children pictured in school textbooks are virtually identical.[31] We have all seen clips of the Arirang mass games in which scores of children of the same height, body type and hairstyle dance and leap in

unison. These games are not the grim Stalinist exercises in anti-individualism that foreigners (such as the makers of the aforementioned documentary) often misperceive them as, but joyous celebrations of the pure-bloodedness and homogeneity from which the race's superiority derives.

The term "military first" does not mean that the armed forces lead the party; rather it is the party which, in accordance with Kim Jong Il's will, puts the military first. It is also the party's own propaganda that puts the armed forces on a high pedestal. Yet this glorification is often so extravagant as to make it appear that the party is abdicating at least part of its traditional role. Visual depictions of the new society tend to show a soldier (massive forearm outstretched, mouth open in a shout) leading the way for factory workers, farmers and scientists. The TV evening news often quotes Kim Jong Il as calling the military "the university of the revolution," and "a magnificent school of ideological, intellectual and physical training."[32] (One wonders where this leaves the nation's women, most of whom do not go through this school.) The soldier is also held up as a model for all to emulate, which is not necessarily the case with the party cadre. (The latter is a much less prominent and heroic figure in North Korean narrative than in the socialist realism of the old East Bloc.)[33] Kim Jong Il is said to "love warriors most of all."[34]

The DPRK's cult of military life is different from its Prussian or Japanese counterparts in that training is seen as going with and not against the grain of the recruit's instincts. Discipline is all well and good, but must never diminish the race's unique spontaneity. Indeed, in one "historical" novel from the 1950s, Kim Il Sung commands the headstrong young protagonist to stay away from the guerilla fighting in the hope that this order will be disregarded![35] The film *The Youths of the SS Seagull* (Kalmaegiho ch'ŏngnyŏndŭl, 1961) invites the audience to side with the boyish hero as he cheerfully flouts the rules of his ship, annoying superiors no end. Needless to say, he does so for the sake of the collective, overstaying his shore leave to win a prize pig for his crewmates' dinner, and so on. Still, such a story would have been inconceivable in the USSR.

Even in war, soldiers are depicted as overgrown children. A tank driver in the story *Tank No. 214* (Ttangk'ŭ 214 ho, 1953):

> The skin was dark, but the face was both noble and adorable, like the face of a small child. Chŏn Ki-ryŏn's expression didn't even change when he rolled over the enemy.... Chŏn was a twenty one year old boy. A voice within Comrade Sŏ suddenly called out, "You kill people with a smile, you little rascal, you were born to beat the enemy!"[36]

For all the army-as-school rhetoric, depictions of life in uniform dwell more on its healthy fraternal joys than its intellectual or physical rigors.[37] Boisterousness is smiled upon as the mark of truly Korean naivety and innocence. In 2006 a magazine article told approvingly of soldiers who vaulted a fence in a mad rush to welcome Kim Jong Il's sedan.[38] There has been no shortage of historical incidents—from the Panmunjom axe-killings of 1976 to the recent shooting of a South Korean tourist at the Kumgangsan resort, to say nothing of the army's maraudings during the famine—which indicate that this celebration of instinctive behavior has affected the culture of the real-life military. This in turn seems to have contributed to a certain friction between the military and the civilian population. At the very least, the latter is not unenvious of the special position accorded to the former. Hence the media's constant and strident emphasis on the need for unity and cooperation between soldiers and civilians.[39]

At the time of writing (autumn 2009), a so-called "100 Day Battle" is in progress. Enthusiasm campaigns to boost production were a fixture in the socialist bloc too, but in North Korea economic growth is less an end in itself than a means to strengthen the country. (The parallel to the German *Wehrwirtschaft* and the Japanese "self-defense state" of the 1930s is obvious.)[40] To get the masses in the proper spirit, the regime compares workers to warriors, and, if the nightly news is anything to go by, hangs signs reading "battleground" in factories.

Whether soldiers, workers or farmers, the heroes in official narratives differ from other characters only in degree: they are that little bit more Korean—more virtuous and pure—than everyone else. Despite the growing focus on the armed forces, which remain predominantly male, young females are still more common in propaganda stories than men. This is not because women are considered fully equal, let alone superior, to men, but because they are more natural symbols of chastity and purity and thus of Koreanness. The most popular character in the peninsula's folk tradition is Ch'unhyang, a girl punished for refusing to yield to a lecherous official. Her story has been filmed several times in North as in South Korea.[41]

Girls have the added advantage of being able to embody both the childlike attitude of the model subject and the nurturing, maternal attitude expected from authority figures. Nurses and female doctors are common heroines. The Text usually shows them as having grown up in fatherless and therefore more spontaneous surroundings. They behave girlishly even in adulthood, blushing at the drop of a hat and covering their mouths when they smile. Squeaky-clean teasing about boyfriends results in giggling mock-chases.[42] One could not be further removed from the tough, emancipated heroines of socialist realist fiction.

Soviet narratives made much of the exertions and austerities of work life, the better to show "the new man" triumphing over his baser urges, but being inherently unselfish, Koreans take pleasure even in the hardest work. Kim Il Sung spoke of the nation's workers as "laboring for the nation and society as well as for their own happiness, taking joy in their labor."[43] Collective farming is presented as the continuation and intensification of the (highly mythologized) Korean tradition of village labor pools.[44] Whether baking in front of a smelting furnace or gripping shovels in the icy cold, workers are usually shown smiling or laughing.[45]

Obligatory in tales of work life are invocations of the campaign slogans of the day, but these tend to be extraneous to variations of the same morality tale about a model worker inspiring his or her comrades, surmounting this or that bureaucratic obstacle or material shortage, and perhaps shaming a mildly bad egg into reform. Since the latter half of the 1980s a whole genre of "hidden hero" narratives has arisen to celebrate those who toil in unglamorous jobs in remote locales. This propaganda is also meant to reconcile the provincial populace to country life and to encourage city women to marry rural husbands. In *City Girl, Come and Get Married* (Tosi ch'ŏnyŏ sijip wayo, 1993), for example, a beauty from Pyongyang falls in love with a duck farmer.[46] But the Text's glorification of country life as the repository of pure ethnic values undoubtedly has much to do with the fact that Korea experienced urbanization at foreign hands; similar tendencies, are obvious in South Korean culture. In Soviet and Chinese narrative, in contrast, the countryside was often depicted as a place of ignorance and reaction.[47]

The explicit ideological content of North Korean narratives has always been much lower than foreigners have assumed. Though often praised in passing, Juche Thought is rarely espoused or explained; having been conceived primarily for the benefit of foreign audiences, its universal-humanist principles—"man is the master of all things," etc—are too difficult to reconcile with the *de facto* ideology of paranoid nationalism. The personality cult is not always front and center either; some movies contain only one or two explicit references to the Leader. Much of the country's visual art may appear completely apolitical to the foreign eye. The North Korean is trained to "read" these works differently. *Happiness* (Haengbok, 1978), for example, shows a girl asleep in bed, her well-groomed head resting on a lace-edged pillow as she clutches a present too precious to unwrap. While the average American may respond by thinking, "Isn't she sweet?" the North Korean is meant to think, "Aren't *our* children sweet?" and "Aren't we lucky to live so well under the Leader?" (For the gift is of course from none other.)

Happiness, 1978

Similarly, every act of kindness depicted is meant to demonstrate the unique goodness of the race. When a mother in the historical film *Sea of Blood* (P'ibada, 1968) skips supper so that her child may eat, much as mothers around the world do every day, the North Korean viewer sheds a tear at the unique intensity of a *Korean* mother's love.[†] The celebration of the race's selflessness routinely trumps the dictates of realism. In one popular movie a KPA soldier with a shattered leg goes under the knife. He worries that he will be crippled for life, but when he wakes up his leg is fine. Wait: the medical staff around him are hobbling! It turns out that they have donated parts of their own flesh and bone to reconstruct his limb.[48]

For decades romance was but the spoonful of sugar helping the propaganda message go down. Now that the party must compete with smuggled South Korean videos and DVD's for public attention, the romantic element has come to the fore, but when one person falls for another, it is usually because the other is such a model citizen. In a television drama broadcast in 2001, an aging bachelor in Pyongyang shows little interest in the young beauty he encounters in a hardware store until he finds out that she has volunteered to work in the same collective potato farm. (Since the launch of the "potato revolution" in the late 1990s, the regime has glorified citizens who relocate to the remote northeastern region where most potatoes are farmed.) He proposes marriage to her that very day, she accepts, and they go off to celebrate with his mother and her aunt. Naturally, no fathers are in sight.[49]

Lovers are rarely shown even touching each other; the Text draws the line at encouraging *adult* instincts. Where the Soviet or Chinese hero's celibacy reflects his total mastery of himself, the North Korean hero's is the cheerful abstinence of the child race. Special pride is taken in the chastity of the peninsula's womenfolk, who in historical narratives are shown

[†]When I was screening the film to my South Korean graduate students, one of them turned smilingly to me during this part and said, "Typical Korean mother!"

fending off lecherous foreigners. Even scenes of childbirth are evidently taboo. To be sure, the more "literary" kind of fiction hints at a sensual element:

> The two walked side by side on the waterway embankment.... Full of merriment Ch'o'ae walked close at Su'ungi's side. He felt as if his heart would burst from his ribs. From Ch'o'ae's slim and firm body, and her soft and gleaming hair, which came down to just below her ears, came a fragrance that chased the smell of dank water far away. Smelling this rich fragrance and feeling her soft body next to his, he walked on, exhilarated. Each was silent, as if trying to hide the excitement bestowed on them by this time together. Only the sound of their footsteps broke the deep silence of the night.[50]

And Hong Sŏk-chung's novel *Hwang Jin'i* (2002), which deals with a famous sixteenth century courtesan of that name, is downright raunchy in parts, but then, more latitude has always been granted to those depicting the decadent, Chinese-influenced "feudal" past. (The book may also have been written with a view to the ROK market.)[51]

But judging from refugee testimony, North Koreans are no fonder of the solitary activity of reading than South Koreans are.[†] Most get their romance from films and TV dramas, which still depict love in a twee and formulaic manner reminiscent of Bollywood, with girlfriends summoned by bird-call imitations, courtship conducted while bobbing around a tree, and so on.[52] The childishness of the love exalts it. As the DPRK's most influential writer once said of his characters, their "love is

[†] In 2005 it was reported that South Koreans read the least (only about three hours a week to Americans' six) among the thirty nations whose consumer habits were surveyed by a consultancy. See "Indians 'world's biggest readers,'" BBC News, June 27, 2005.

permeated with Korean morality, in contrast to the greasy love of Western people."[53] What may look to outsiders like a simple love story is thus as much a part of the Text as everything else.

While the party does not explicitly deny the existence of conflict inside the republic, it contends that conflict is not "typical" of North Korean life and therefore unworthy of depiction. There are few of the harsh clashes between rural and urban values, older and younger generations, chauvinist husbands and progressive wives, etc, that were so common in Soviet propaganda. Though divorce and light spousal abuse have ceased to be taboo topics, they are attributed to such innocuous reasons as one partner's excessive dedication to the workplace: "You only know about production, not about living," complains the wife in the TV drama *Family* (Kajŏng, 2001).[54]

Mid-level bureaucrats are sometimes criticized as a social class, but individual North Koreans are never singled out as true villains. (The media, for their part, never report on crimes committed in the DPRK; since the 1960s, victims of political purges have simply become non-people.) There are, however, plenty of mildly flawed individuals to be found in narratives: girls who spend too much time on their appearance, say, or men who "abandon" their mountain village to chase dreams of life in the city. Being Korean and thus inherently virtuous, these characters are easily reformed. A soldier who fails to sweep the floor of his tent sees that a comrade has done the job for him—and bursts into tears of repentance. (This plot device is now so stale that even Kim Jong Il has complained about it.)[55] As a result, a serene and idyllic quality attaches to most portrayals of contemporary life. Depictions of the food shortage treat it, as we shall see in a later chapter, as a period of dramatic belt-tightening that is now over and done with. When storytellers want to criticize downright illegal or subversive activity they must resort to fables or cartoons with animal figures. (This is one reason why the North's animation industry is so advanced.) A warning against fleeing to China, for example, is expressed as a tale of a squirrel who ventures too far abroad.[56]

The lack of conflict makes North Korean narratives seem dull even in comparison to Soviet fiction. Rather than try to stimulate curiosity about what will happen next, directors and writers try to make one wonder what has already happened. Films introduce characters in a certain situation (getting a medal, say), then go back and forth in time to explain how they got there.[57] Nowhere in the world do writers make such heavy use of the flashback. But we should beware of assuming that people in the DPRK find these narratives as dull as we do. The Korean aesthetic has traditionally been very tolerant of convention and formula. (South Korean broadcasters re-work the same few soap-opera plots every year.) According to refugee testimony, however, most North Koreans prefer stories set either in the "Yankee colony" or in pre-revolutionary times, with real villains and conflict.

The country's favorite movie, by all accounts, is *The Flower Girl* (Kkot' p'anŭn ch'ŏnyŏ, 1972), which was filmed a few years after the staging of a "revolutionary opera"— allegedly penned by Kim Il Sung in his youth—under the same title.[†] The virginal heroine's white-bloused form graces the republic's currency, and she is routinely invoked by bachelors as the kind of woman they want to marry. (Some credit for the character's appeal must go to the beautiful Hong Myŏng-hŭi, who acted the part while still a teenager.) Set in the colonial era and filmed in nightmarish Technicolor,

From *The Flower Girl*, 1972.

[†] It is claimed that Kim Il Sung conceived and staged the story in Manchuria during the anti-Japanese struggle, but the fact that it was not mentioned until the 1960s, when Mao's international fame as a poet was burgeoning, speaks for itself.

the film follows its flower-selling heroine as she weeps her way through one family crisis after the other: her brother is dragged away by the police, her little sister blinded by the landlady, her mother worked to death, etc. Everything from the heartbreak-laden plot to the flower-girl motif reflects the influence of the Japanese schmaltz (itself influenced by Victorian England) which dominated Korean theaters during the colonial period.[†]

At last the girl's brother, having escaped from prison and joined Kim Il Sung's partisans, returns to exact revenge on the landlord. Although the heroine pledges to join the revolutionary struggle, it is not her sudden access of fighting spirit but the purity and naivety that she displays throughout the film that have made her an ethnic icon. This, the movie says, is how hard it was to be Korean in this evil world—before the Leader set the race free.

[†] Popular "new kabuki" plays performed by visiting Japanese troupes in the 1910s and 1920s helped to engender a Korean tradition of weepy and formulaic "sinp'agŭk" narratives, the influence of which can be seen in South Korean films and TV serials even today. Ho, Han'guk yŏnghwa 100-nyŏn, 22-24.

CHAPTER THREE
THE PARENT LEADER

Western journalists routinely claim that North Korea is essentially a Confucian country.[1] A "Confucian version of George Orwell's 1984," writes one, a "Confucian museum, covered by a thick but superficial layer of Marxism-Leninism," writes another.[2] Scholars such as Selig Harrison and Thomas Hosuck Kang agree that the regime's longevity can be attributed in large part to its skill in exploiting this age-old tradition.[3] In fact the DPRK's official culture clashes with the sage's teachings in all significant respects. Confucius demanded rigorous self-cultivation through study; the Kim regime urges its subjects to remain as childlike and spontaneous as possible. Confucius considered no race better than another; the DPRK regards the Korean people as uniquely virtuous. Nor does the Workers' Party condone the rites of ancestor worship that are still taken so seriously in the southern half of the peninsula.

To most observers, the North Korean regime's heavy use of family symbolism is sufficient proof of Confucian tendencies. But almost all cultures espouse respect for one's parents, and kinship metaphors have been part of political language since time immemorial. Indeed, there was once a father figure in every communist country. In order to prove a Confucian influence on the DPRK's personality cult, one would have to demonstrate that there is something *distinctly* Confucian about it, a task doomed to failure. Contrary to what so many outsiders take for granted, the leader depicted in official propaganda is hardly a father figure at all, let alone a patriarch.

Before discussing this any further, let us summarize the current version of Kim Il Sung's mythobiography.[†]

[†] I say "current," because the myths have changed over the decades. It was not until the mid-1960s, for example, that the Text began claiming Kim Il Sung had defeated the Japanese and the Americans without foreign assistance.

On April 15 in 1912, the first year of Juche, in the Man'gyŏngdae district of Pyongyang, a son was born to Kim Hyŏng-jik and his wife Kang Pan-sŏk. It quickly became clear to all in the village that this was no ordinary child; more upright and virtuous than his playmates, he climbed a tree in a naïve effort to catch the rainbow. When only seven, he saw the police arrest his father for anti-Japanese activities. After his release in 1923 the family resolved to leave for Manchuria. Mature beyond his years, the boy vowed not to return to Pyongyang until Korea's independence had been restored.

In Manchuria Kim Il Sung devoted himself wholly to the anti-Japanese struggle. By the age of sixteen he had already formed the Anti-Imperialist League and purged the Korean revolutionary movement of narrow-minded nationalists and xenophiles alike. At a conference of revolutionaries in 1930 the eighteen-year-old Kim set out his brilliant new ideology of Juche Thought, explaining that man is the master of all things, and that a revolutionary strategy for Korea must reflect the country's unique conditions. Two years later he founded the Korean People's Revolutionary Army. Basing his headquarters first in the Tumen River region, then on sacred Mount Paektu, he launched a series of crushing attacks on Japanese troops. After a particularly bold strike on the Korean border town of Pochǒnbo in 1937 the KPRA found itself under threat from a counter-offensive. Kim rescued his troops in the winter of 1938/39 by leading them on the now-legendary Arduous March along the Yalu River valley. Not once did he rest or slacken in his concern for his men, who under his brilliant leadership won every battle. In 1942 his wife Kim Chǒng-suk, a revolutionary fighter since childhood, bore the General a son. The couple named him Jong Il.

On August 9, 1945, the General led his army in a final concerted push through the enemy's border strongholds, at the same time ordering secret fighting units to rise up across the peninsula. The Japanese held out for all of six days before falling to their knees on August 15. As the victorious army advanced southward people rushed weeping from their homes to greet its commander. Arriving at last in Pyongyang, Kim restored its ancient status as the nation's capital by setting up his government there.

Alas, the American imperialists had already invaded the southern part of the peninsula, installing the reactionary Syngman Rhee as "president" of the new colony. On June 25, 1950 the Yankees, determined to crush Korean socialism forever, launched a surprise attack on the DPRK. Under the General's brilliant leadership, the Korean People's Army dealt them such a savage series of counter-blows that they retreated whence they came, finally signing an abject declaration of surrender on July 27, 1953.

In the years that followed Kim Il Sung worked day and night, waking every morning at 3 am as he rebuilt his country into a shining model of self-reliant independence. Juche Study groups sprang up around the world as foreigners sought to emulate the DPRK's spectacular progress in all fields. But for all his many duties, the Leader found time to visit factories and farms, solving their problems at lightning speed while touching the hearts of the workers with his parental concern for their welfare. Unfortunately this selflessness took a toll on his health, and on July 8 1994 he passed away, plunging the masses into a grief such as they had never known. It was no small comfort for them, however, to know that the Dear Leader Kim Jong Il would carry on his father's legacy.[4]

Although the DPRK came close to another war with the US in the last years of Kim Il Sung's life, the resolution of this crisis is generally credited to his son, who by then had assumed command of the armed forces. Yet the summary above should not mislead anyone into thinking that the personality

Visual documents of pre-liber-
ation history hardly look like
photographs at all, though they
are referred to as such. Left: Kim
Il Sung as a schoolboy in exile.
Right: Kim with his wife, Kim
Chŏng-suk, in their guerrilla days.
The crudeness of these forgeries
is no mere matter of technical in-
eptitude; a country that can forge
US currency can do much better
than this. The regime seems to
want to present its creation myth
as a grand, epic past that must be
believed on its own terms.

The Torch of Poch'ŏnbo (1948), one of the earliest pictorial depictions of
Kim Il Sung, shows the "general" and his guerrillas after their famous victory
against a Japanese border outpost. While the battle itself is recorded fact,
the quality of the uniforms shown here attests to the personality cult's indifference to the dictates of realism.

Kim Il Sung, his wife Kim Jong Suk and their son Kim Jong Il ride horses near the liberation army's secret camp on Mount Paektu. Note how the color of the uniforms differs from the earlier depiction.

Kim Il Sung greets the adoring masses; behind him, the DPRK's coat of
arms, a red star shining down on a hydroelectric power plant. The personality
cult has never hid the corpulence of either of the Kims; on the contrary, it is
seen as a sign of their spontaneous and easy-going nature. Yankee villains, in
contrast, are often beanpole-thin.

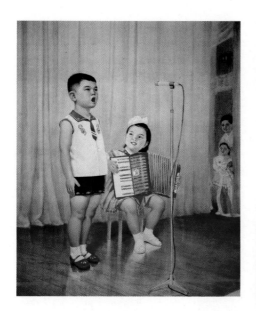

Left: Kim Il Sung "visits kindergarten in a mountain village." Propaganda likes to associate both leaders with snow, a symbol of purity, and with carefree children, symbols of the innocent spontaneity of the race.

Above: Kim Il Sung "visits a school on the first day of compulsory 11-year education." Here too the leader seems not to be talking at all, instead simply exuding benevolent solicitude and good cheer; this is no traditional Confucian educator, let alone a Marxist-Leninist one à la Stalin or Mao, but an indulgent parent on the side of the instincts.

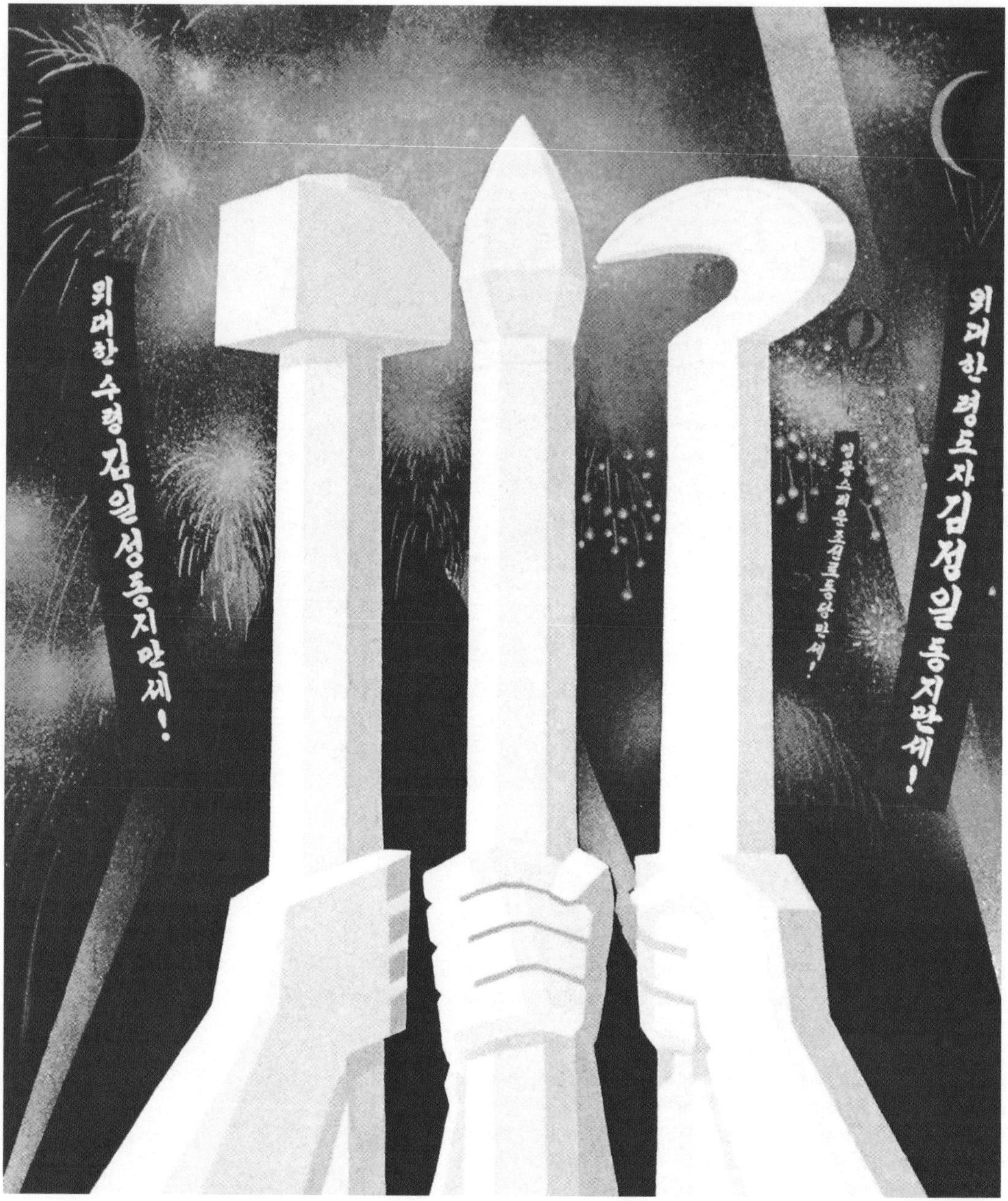
위대한 수령 김일성동지만세!
영광스러운조선로동당만세!
위대한 령도자 김정일 동지만세!

Above: Kim Il Sung on one of his countless "on-the-spot guidance" visits. (In his depiction of the leader's coat and hat, the artist has rather unwisely worked from a real photograph.) These visits, as the written records of them make clear, are not about imparting knowledge or revolutionary consciousness; the content of Kim's guidance is less important than the trouble he took—often, as here, in the dead of winter—to administer it.

Left: The Workers' Party symbol shows a hoe for farm laborers, a hammer for industrial workers, and (a rarity in the symbols of socialist parties) a writing brush for the higher-educated or white collar class. This last has helped keep casual foreign observers from recognizing the DPRK's intense anti-intellectualism.

Above: Kim Jong Il is often depicted as having spent his school years in the 1950s enlightening fellow students about his father's Juche Thought. In fact, the sham doctrine was not even spoken of until the cultural revolution of the mid-1960s, with the first books on the subject appearing several years after that.

Left: While some landscapes are painted in a kitschy, extravagant manner, others, like this one, are done in a more subdued and traditional style. Either way, what is celebrated is not nature in general but the nature of the motherland. With its rugged, lofty peaks and pure mountain streams, the Korean landscape is thought to reflect the characteristics of the race itself.

Demobilized soldiers, still carrying their military-issue knapsacks, are welcomed with flowers by the workplace to which they have been assigned. While Soviet painters played up the heroic exertions and sacrifices of industrial laborers, the better to show them "tempering" their spontaneity, the DPRK's propaganda depicts collective work as something joyful to which Koreans are instinctively inclined.

Kim Jong Il comforts a distraught nation after his father's death on July 8, 1994. In the background is the 66 ft. high bronze statue of the Great Leader that was erected on Mansu Hill in Pyongyang in 1972. Dark skies in depictions of this period symbolize the growing threat from without.

The myth of Kim's tireless, never-ending inspection of the country's defenses is meant to absolve him of responsibility for the DPRK's economic woes.

The Dear Leader stands guard as the waves of a hostile world crash ineffectually against the rocks.

Kim Jong Il and Bill Clinton pose for a photograph after their meeting on August 4, 2009. The choice of background was no accident: waves breaking on the rocky coast symbolize the futility of the world's harassment of the motherland.

South Korean cooperation with the North is often misrepresented as a shared effort to drive out the American enemy, shown here in standard hook-nosed form. The legend reads: "Working together as national brethren, let's reckon with the US imperialists and unite Korea!"

우리 당의 선군혁명령도를 충성으로 받들자!

Since the proclamation of a "military-first" policy in 1995, the Supreme Commander's five-pointed star has become as prominent a propaganda motif as the national flag itself. Standard are depictions of a square-jawed soldier leading the way to a strong and prosperous country, while the rest of society—here a laborer and a white collar worker with one of Kim Jong Il's works—follows closely behind. But outsiders who think the military has been placed over the party should note that the legend reads, "Let us loyally venerate *the party's* military-first leader-ship." (Emphasis mine) It is the party, in other words, that puts the military first.

In a depiction of the near future, joyous Koreans praise Kim Jong Il for having brought about national reunification. The vertical banner over the peninsula reads: "Long live General Kim, the Sun of Unification!"

For decades South Korea was depicted as the "living hell" to the North's "paradise on earth"; the collapse of the information cordon in the mid-1990s made the regime take a more nuanced propaganda line.

cult skims over the latter half of the Great Leader's life. The problem, for my purposes at least, is that only the first half forms a linear story. The second falls apart into undated tales of "on-the-spot guidance" and other anecdotes that are too numerous to count, let alone summarize. They play such an important role in official myth that new ones are constantly being generated.[5]

A personality cult comes into being when a one-man dictatorship presents itself as a democracy. The goal is to convey the impression that due to the ruler's unique qualifications and the unanimity of the people's love for him, his rule constitutes the perfect fulfillment of democratic ideals. In this respect at least, the Kim cult resembles the cults of Mao and Stalin. In most others it is closer to the leader cults of fascism. Where the Chinese and Soviet cults derived their respective leaders' greatness from an unequalled grasp of dialectical materialism, the North Korean cult derives Kim's from his embodiment of ethnic virtues: he is the most naïve, spontaneous, loving, and pure Korean—the most Korean Korean—who ever lived. As one propagandist recently put it, "Kim Il Sung is the symbol of the homeland."[6]

To eliminate all doubt that the Leader's virtues were inborn and not acquired, the Text plays up his impeccable lineage (crediting his great-grandfather with leading a famous attack on an American gunship in 1866) and the very young age at which he began manifesting his virtue.[7] His father Kim Hyŏng-jik (a rather pallid hero of the resistance for whom the Text can work up no real passion) is rarely shown teaching his son, let alone disciplining him.[8] With very short hair and a soft, pale-moon face marked by small and feminine features, the boy Kim recalls the children pictured in imperial Japanese schoolbooks. Usually he looks cheerful, showing the dimpled smile to which the Text constantly draws attention. In some pictures, like one in which he receives a gun from his mother, he seems to sense the responsibility weighing on his young shoulders, but even here his eyes are blank: because true Korean spontaneity ends where an intellectual expression begins, Kim is never shown *thinking*.[9] Anything that might be

Blank-eyed as always, the young Kim takes from his mother the gun with which he would start his war of liberation.

seen as having diminished the leader's artlessness and naivety is downplayed or ignored altogether. Love of the race leads him spontaneously to Marxism, an ideology that the Text praises but (for obvious reasons) is loath to explain.

One may well ask how a leader can pose as the embodiment of naivety on the one hand and a brilliant strategist and revolutionary on the other. In the 1940s and 1950s writers made ludicrous efforts to explain away this contradiction, claiming, among other things, that Kim's best ideas came to him in his sleep.[10] The propaganda apparatus soon realized it would be better simply to divert public attention elsewhere. While the leader's genius and invincibility on the battlefield are accorded all due praise, only his ethnic virtues—his naivety, his purity, his spontaneity and solicitude—are constantly shown in action.

In depictions of his guerilla years, for example, the young General is almost never seen in actual combat. Instead he appears between battles, fussing cheerfully over his soldiers' food and well being.[11] His wife Kim Chŏng-suk, the object of her own minor personality cult, cuts a more martial figure than he does. She is even referred to as his "bodyguard."[12] In one illustration she sternly holds back her smooth-faced husband while she fires at the Japanese enemy.[13]

How, the critical outsider may ask, did the General manage to keep his guerillas so well-dressed and well-armed? If he never lost a battle, why was almost no Korean territory liberated until that effortless "final push"? Why is *every* photograph from this period so blurred and grainy?[14] Citizens born in the DPRK might not wonder about such things, but what about those old enough to have experienced the Soviet occupation? We can, I believe, exclude the possibility that they swallowed the new version of history whole, rejecting their own memories in the process. More likely they shrugged off its "mere" factual inaccuracies while accepting it as essentially true. Foreigners fought the Japanese out of imperialist motives no better than Japan's; only Koreans fought for pure and righteous reasons; ergo only the Korean fight was historically meaningful. South Korean nationalists interpret modern history in much the same way.

Confident of the popular desire to believe in a homegrown liberation army, the propaganda apparatus has never worried much about realism or consistency. For a while it was claimed that the revolutionary army had acquired its gleaming weapons by sneaking up on Japanese sentries and throwing red pepper in their eyes![15] Over the past sixty years the young Kim and his fighters have been depicted in lavish uniforms of various styles and colors, an olive-brown finally replacing the too Japanese-looking khaki of old.[16] The foreigner may well chuckle at this, as at the other preposterous illustrations in the history books: the General's pristine log cabin, looking like something in a child's snow-dome; demure female partisans dashing through emerald forests in crisply pleated skirts. But there is more method here than meets the eye. The liberation myth would not exert as strong an appeal if it were served cold, i.e., as a sober and realistic narrative of an all-too recent history. The regime wisely prefers to depict a magical and epic past that must be accepted on its own terms.

Needless to say, the Text claims that Kim Il Sung took over the country on the day of liberation, August 15, 1945, though it fails to explain why two months elapsed before his triumphant homecoming speech to an enormous Pyongyang crowd. This event is the subject of many verbal and visual depictions, all of them far removed from the original photograph taken that October 14, which has been doctored beyond recognition. (The Soviet generals who stood directly behind Kim at the rally are nowhere to be seen; neither is the Red Army medal on his chest.)[17] Paintings of the first months of independence often show Kim at the center of a frantically cheering crowd. Sometimes he wears a dark suit, sometimes a military-type uniform with knee-high white padded boots, sometimes a white tunic and matching trousers.[18] Another popular theme is his triumphant return to Man'gyŏngdae, the village of his childhood. We are meant to marvel at the great man's humility as he chats with straight-talking aunts and uncles.[19]

In contrast to depictions of the guerilla era, Kim appears in DPRK-themed pictures always as plump, if never quite as fat as he was in real life. Unlike Stalin and Mao, who personified the triumph of consciousness over the instincts, Kim had little need to pose as an ascetic. On the contrary, his plumpness symbolizes the race's newfound freedom to indulge its innocent instincts. (Yankee villains, incidentally, are beanpole thin.)[20]

The DPRK's propagandists are clearly uncomfortable with the "Homeland Liberation War," even if they do depict it as a glorious victory over the US; there is no getting around the awkward fact that the republic was utterly devastated on the Parent Leader's watch. War writers thus tend to keep him off-stage while invoking him as a galvanizing inspiration to the race. Soldiers shout "Long Live General Kim Il Sung" as they lead the charge or blow themselves up in suicide attacks.[21] One of the few well-known war-themed works in which Kim makes a physical appearance is a painting

entitled "Leader, the Front Line is Up Ahead." Kim has just
disembarked from the presidential jeep (bearing, in cap and
jackboots, an unfortunate resemblance to a chauffeur). While
an aide surveys the smoke-dimmed middle distance, a female
soldier—the usual bob-haired personification of Korean
chastity—informs the leader that the front is just around the
bend. Kim, somehow standing atop the thick mud and not in
it, listens with a smile. Presumably one is meant to marvel at
his courage in putting himself so close to harm's way and his
modesty in traveling with only one aide.[22]

In depictions of the post-war years—or the Homeland Reconstruction Period, as it is called—the Great Leader is again in the forefront, often dressed in purifying white as he conducts "on-the-spot guidance" at farms, factories and construction sites. The Text gushes endlessly about these visits. Many of them were reported on days after they allegedly took place, and are remembered today with plaques and stone slabs, some engraved in blood-red script, at the relevant sites. (In 2008 I saw a South Korean tourist sternly rebuked for touching one of them.) But quite a few depictions of Kim's "on-the-spot guidance" are presented to the public *as* literature and art, as works of the imagination. The leader's statements in such stories are therefore not printed in boldface, as they would have to be if the account were ostensibly true.†

Their air of intimacy removes all doubt that they are fictional: no North Korean would think that a mere writer could have been privy to the great man's private thoughts and conversations. Lest anyone still contrive to miss the point, these accounts are published as "short fiction" (tanp'yŏn sosŏl) and reviewed accordingly, with critics either praising or—much less often—faulting a writer for the story he has dreamed up.[23] The reader is nonetheless expected to believe that the work is true to the *essence* of the great man. (A comparison can be made to the non-Biblical tales of Jesus taught to Christian children.) With paintings it is somewhat harder to tell imaginary scenes from purportedly historical ones, though the latter are more likely to include dates and locations in their titles.[24]

It may seem odd that such a repressive regime would allow writers and artists to cast the leader in situations of their own

†The bold-print rule applies to all ostensibly authentic statements from Kim Il Sung, his parents, his wife and (of course) his son Jong Il.

imagining, but only the most trusted members of the cultural apparatus are commissioned to create such works. In doing so they must not only meet the party's demands for a certain topical theme—a campaign to boost agricultural production may call for depiction of the leader at a farm—but also follow the Text's rigid iconography. Artists, for example, must copy the face already familiar from canonical pictures; there are none of the minor stylistic variations evident in Soviet paintings of Stalin or Lenin.

Stories of Kim's "on-the-spot guidance" are alike not only in their depiction of the hero, but in their storylines and secondary characters as well. The latter usually include a rather slow-witted aide—a different man each time, the better to play up his comic astonishment at the leader's every word and deed. Things usually start off with Kim in an unidentified office. (In contrast to the Stalin cult, with its many paeans to the "light in the Kremlin window," the Text does not associate the leader with any particular residence or workplace; he was and is everywhere, for he is at the heart of every Korean.) The standard plot: the aide reports on a problem in a remote farm or factory, the leader jovially suggests a road trip, and the two men head out in the presidential sedan, throwing everyone into a tizzy when they arrive. The leader must then be shown solving the problem, but without coming off as cerebral and therefore un-Korean. Both problem and solution are thus described in terms a child can grasp.

Indeed, the Leader's published remarks are *always* trite: "Rainbow trout is a good fish, tasty and nutritious."[25] Foreigners who mock these platitudes fail to realize that the content of Kim's guidance is not as important as the time and effort he takes to administer it. (In many pictures of these visits, he is merely listening with a smile.²⁶) After all, to impart consciousness and discipline to the child race would be to make it less pure and childlike, which must never happen. Nor could Kim pose as an educator or disciplinarian without seeming an imperfect embodiment of Koreanness. In short stories, the emotional climax comes *after* Kim's breezy solution of the problem, usually in a scene in which he fusses over someone in the adoring throng who looks cold or tired.²⁷ It is this loving attentiveness on the part of the world's busiest man that moves the characters to tears, and is meant to make the reader cry too. Even when Kim is referred to as Father Leader (*abŏji suryŏng*), therefore, there is nothing Confucian or patriarchal about him. In a short story called "Father," for example, he neither exercises authority nor imparts wisdom, but rushes an injured child to hospital. The official encyclopedia praises the story in maternal terms, describing "the Great General as the loving parent who holds and nurtures all Korean children at his breast."²⁸

Note the pointedly androgynous or—more accurately— hermaphroditic designation of "parent." Kim is referred to primarily as Parent Leader (*ŏbŏi suryŏng*), though with his maternal side praised far more often than the other.²⁹ Kim Jong Il himself has long described his father's motherly qualities as key to his success. These qualities manifested themselves "even in his teenage years."

> Like a sensitive and meticulous mother the Leader took it upon himself to know people through and through, and to make them feel better with just one word, so it is only natural that everyone believed in the leader and followed him.³⁰

Artists and writers not only play up the feminine aspects of Kim Il Sung's appearance—the soft, pale face, the dimpled smile, the expansive bosom—but also show him holding small children or letting them clamber over him. In photographs we see him grinning as schoolgirls pull yearningly on his arms and hands.[31] Even in depictions of his guerilla years these qualities are always on display. In one illustration he is tucking children into bed. The title of another, "The Parent Leader General Kim Il Sung Holding the Children of Mt. Ma'an to his Breast," speaks for itself.[32]

But even grown Koreans are children at heart, and to be treated accordingly. Here is the first verse from the song "The Leader Came to the Sentry Post":

The Leader came all the way to the sentry post
And held us affectionately to his bosom
So happy about the warm love he bestowed on us
We buried our faces in his bosom
Ah! He is our parent!
Ah! A son in his embrace
Is happy always, everywhere![33]

In one painting Kim smilingly squats down in deep snow, tying a young soldier's bootlaces; in another he drapes an overcoat over an exhausted cadre who has fallen asleep at his desk.[34] In "Worrying About A Warrior's Health," the smiling Kim is holding to his chest a young soldier, who like a child has pressed his pink-cheeked face up against the white tunic.[35]

Though all personality cults stress the people's love for their leader, the North Korean one differs from its Soviet and

Chinese counterparts in stressing individual citizens' personal yearning to see him or be held in his embrace. "I miss the General" is a constant refrain. The chorus of the plaintive official classic "Where Are You, General I Long For?" runs, "The harder the cold autumn wind blows/ the more I yearn for the warm bosom of the General."[36]

The closest Kim Il Sung comes to appearing as a father in more than name is when he is depicted together with Kim Jong Il. The reason is obvious: If the Great Leader were shown mothering his own son, the public might be inclined to conclude that the latter had a privileged upbringing, a notion the regime—as we shall see in the following chapter—is at constant pains to dispel. Paintings often show the older man walking with dignified mien a pace ahead of the younger one, much as one sees real-life fathers and sons walking in South Korean corporations.[37] The younger man must of course be shown learning from his father, because the hereditary succession derives its legitimacy in no small part from the claim that he imbibed Juche from the source. But the Text prefers to show him reflecting vaguely on past lessons; this obviates scenes of father-son instruction in which Kim Il Sung might come off as erudite and therefore un-Korean.

Whether the backdrop is the 1950s or the 1980s, the depiction of the Great Leader is basically the same, though he is shown growing fatter with age, and as an elderly if unwrinkled man is often pictured in black-framed glasses and a cap.[38] (Needless to say, the goiter that afflicted the real-life man in later life is not to be seen either in photographs, which had to be taken from the same angle, or in portraits.) Relaxed and cheerful, he is occasionally even shown with a cigarette in one hand.[39]

A central theme of depictions of the latter half of Kim's rule is his worldwide renown, which brings statesmen from around the world on tributary visits to Pyongyang. He receives them straight-backed, with benign smiles but no real warmth. While all may derive benefit from his insights, his love is for the pure race alone.[40] Special treatment is shown to foreigners who have done the DPRK a particularly great service. "I am grateful to you," Kim tells an obsequious Reverend Billy Graham in a recent account, "for spreading so much propaganda about us."[41]

The Kim of the early 1990s—that is, of the last years of his life—is shown in somewhat different terms. He remains the revered leader of the country, in which role he accepts Jimmy Carter's abject surrender proposal in June 1994, but with his own race run, he is content to leave the defense of the country to his brilliant son.[42] This hereditary succession is seen overseas as proof positive of the DPRK's Confucian tendencies. In depictions of the early 1990s, however, Kim treats his son with a deference that turns the most important of Confucius's Five Relationships on its head. An official documentary made in 1992 shows him writing a florid panegyric to Jong Il, and in historical novels he converses with him, even in private, in polite Korean, addressing him as Supreme Commander or General.[43] When I show these works to my South Korean students, who unlike their northern counterparts have been raised to think in Confucian terms, they laugh and shake their heads.

This does not mean that the Kim cult bears no traces of Korea's pre-colonial traditions, nor that it is completely unlike its defunct Eastern European counterparts. The far more obvious and significant influence, however, is that of the Japanese emperor cult. Like Kim, Hirohito appeared as the hermaphroditic parent of a child race whose virtues he embodied; was associated with white clothing, white horses, the snow-capped peak of the race's sacred mountain, and other symbols of racial purity; was said to be joined with his subjects as one entity, "one mind united from top to bottom"; and referred to as the Sun of the Nation (minjok ŭi t'aeyang), the Great Marshal (taewŏnsu) whom citizens must "venerate" (pattŭlda) and be ready to die for.[44] A significant difference is that while the Text likes to draw bemused attention to outsiders, including Americans and South Koreans, who allegedly regard Kim Il Sung as a divine being, it never makes such claims for him itself.[†] But the similarity between the two cults remains too great to be explained away, as it is by some observers, in terms of borrowed "elements."[45] They are *fundamentally* alike, because they derive from a fundamentally similar view of the world.

Many in the West, of course, continue to doubt that the North Koreans really believe in their personality cult. This skepticism derives in part from recollections of the double lives led in the old East Bloc, where the average educated citizen feigned fervent support for his country's leader in formal settings only to joke about him behind closed doors. But this only goes to show how little the East Bloc and North Korea ever had in common, for the masses' adoration of Kim Il Sung has always been very real. Even among the few North Koreans who have left the country and stayed out, a heartfelt admiration for the Great Leader is mainstream. (I personally know migrants who still cannot talk of him without tearing

[†] In an article entitled "Brilliant Life Dedicated to Country and Nation," it is written, "A foreigner said that...he believed in Kim Il Sung like God. [sic]" KCNA, July 6, 2007. Propaganda about the Dear Leader is similar: it is reported that many foreigners and religious South Koreans regard him as God/a god. In the novel *Gun Barrel* for example, a visiting American concludes that Kim Jong Il is the Messiah. Many foreign researchers mistakenly believe that the North Koreans themselves acclaim their leader as a God. See for example Noland, *Avoiding the Apocalypse*, 62. See also Ch'ongddae, 2003, page 462.

up.) This has much to do with the far greater psychological appeal of nationalism itself, but Kim Il Sung's peculiarly androgynous or hermaphroditic image also seems to exert a far more emotional attraction than any of the unambiguously paternal leaders of Eastern Europe were able to. I am not qualified to analyze the cult (or anything else) from a psychological standpoint, but just enough should be written here to counter the reader's skepticism that sane people could give themselves over to the adoration of a male mother figure. Sigmund Freud wrote of every child's yearning for a phallic mother, a truly omnipotent parent who is both sexes in one, and Ernest Becker agreed that the hermaphroditic image answers a striving for ontological wholeness that is inherent to man.[46] This may explain why Jesus and Buddha are far more feminine and maternal figures in the popular imagination than in the original scriptures of Christianity and Buddhism. The North Koreans' race theory gives them extra reason to want a leader who is both mother enough to indulge their unique childlikeness and father enough to protect them from the evil world.

Interestingly enough, the absence of a patriarchal authority figure may also have helped the regime preserve stability by depriving people of a target to rebel against. C. Fred Alford has written, "In 'society without the father'... everything just is, naturelike in its givenness, so that it does not even occur to one to rebel, just as one does not rebel against the mist."[47] Perhaps it is no wonder that the propaganda apparatus decided to make the country's next leader even more of a mother than Kim Il Sung had been.

CHAPTER FOUR
THE DEAR LEADER

Regardless of whether Kim Jong Il ever intended to pose as his father's equal, the DPRK's fall from Soviet-subsidized grace in the early 1990s made such a strategy impracticable. The Text implicitly admits, therefore, that although the Dear Leader is the greatest man alive, he is not quite the man the Great Leader was. When *père* and *fils* are pictured together in paintings the focal point is always the older, taller, better-looking man.[1] Where Kim Il Sung was the effortless master of *all* sectors of

public life, his son is the military-first "General," compelled by the Yankee threat to concentrate on national defense at the expense of economic matters. Since this is not a Marxist-Leninist state committed to the improvement of material living standards, but rather a nationalist one in which the leader's main function is to embody Korean virtues—which are not seen to include intellectual brilliance anyway—the relative inferiority of Kim Jong Il's genius troubles propagandists less than an outsider might assume. It is in no small part *because* he appears more human and vulnerable than Kim Il Sung, and thus a more convincing embodiment of the child race itself, that the Dear Leader is so dear to his people, even if he is not as fervently venerated as his father.

We already saw that the Text recounts only Kim Il Sung's life before 1945 as a coherent story, reducing the history of his rule to a jumble of "on-the-spot guidance" anecdotes. It does the opposite with the Kim Jong Il cult, telescoping the man's younger years while treating his rule as a linear legend in progress. The mythobiography can be summarized as follows:

It was on February 16 1942, in a snowcapped log cabin at Kim Il Sung's guerilla base on Mount Paektu, that Kim Chŏng-suk gave birth to the Dear Leader Kim Jong Il. Overjoyed partisans celebrated the great event by carving his name into thousands of tree trunks. Although the little boy was often cold and hungry, he never complained, anxious even at that age not to trouble his parents. Alas, no sooner had the Great Leader succeeded in liberating the nation than his loyal wife, weakened by decades of self-sacrifice, fell seriously ill. She passed away in 1949. Before her son had overcome this blow, he was forced to witness first-hand the destruction caused by the American invasion. The experience left him with a lasting hatred of Yankee imperialism. Never one to seek special treatment, he participated directly in the reconstruction of Pyongyang before entering Kim Il Sung University in 1960, where he organized fellow students into Juche study groups.

At the age of 22 he went to work in the party's central committee. For decades he played a vital role in the implementation of the Great Leader's policies and issued brilliant treatises on the Juchefication of the arts. All the while he traveled ceaselessly to farms, factories and military bases around the country, bestowing his motherly love on the masses and earning their love in return.

In the early 1990s the USSR surrendered to the forces of imperialism without a shot. Emboldened, the Yankees stepped up efforts to destroy Korean-style socialism, claiming a non-

existent "nuclear problem" as a pretext for imposing suffocating sanctions on the DPRK. In response Kim Jong Il, who in 1991 had become Supreme Commander of the Korean People's Army, rallied the troops in a spectacular show of resolve, at the same time dispatching diplomatic warriors around the world to make clear that the DPRK would never back down.

In July 1994 Kim Il Sung passed away, plunging the entire nation into mourning. Though his heart was breaking, Kim Jong Il manfully hid his grief from the masses. Again the Yankees smelled victory. Boastfully predicting that the DPRK would not survive for long without the Great Leader, they redoubled their efforts to crush Korean-style socialism. To make matters worse, a freakish combination of natural disasters destroyed one harvest after another. Though in dire straits the masses never complained, trusting instead that the Dear Leader would lead them through this second Arduous March just as his father had led partisans through the first. Aware that the Yankees would stop at nothing, the General announced a military-first government and embarked on a ceaseless tour of army outposts. Wherever he went he moved soldiers to tears by insisting on eating the same meager fare as they.

By the end of the 1990s the worst was over. With a renewed joy and confidence sweeping the nation, the General ushered in a glorious new era by announcing the "Strong and Prosperous Nation" campaign. Shortly thereafter he concluded an agreement with the southern masses to expedite unification by strengthening economic and cultural ties. But that was not all: in 2006 the Dear General successfully oversaw the acquisition of a nuclear deterrent that would protect the Korean race forever. Truly, the son had proven himself worthy of his great father.[2]

Although the regime uses the title "Dear Leader" in English publications, a practice I reluctantly follow in this book, the Korean original should more accurately be translated as "Dear Ruler," for it is not the word "great" but the word "leader" (*suryŏng*) that is reserved for his father; Kim Jong Il is often called Great Ruler (*widaehan yŏngdoja*), as he was in North Korean coverage of his meeting with Bill Clinton in August 2009.

But as the reader can gather from the foregoing summary, there is much more common ground between the myths of the two Kims than there are significant differences. Like his father before him, the Dear Leader embodies Korean virtues and is therefore the greatest man alive. (He too was born with these virtues, as the talk of his angelic toddlerhood is meant to attest.) But to counter the assumption that the boy had an easy time growing up, the Text stresses that he was "born and bred in... difficult circumstances,"[3] extracting plenty of pathos from the death of his young mother: "No matter how he called and cried, [she] still did not come home."[4] Tales abound of his aversion to receiving special treatment.[5] In one novel it is claimed that he always called Kim Il Sung "Leader," "General," etc, refusing to claim special filial status for himself.[6] He is often shown fussing over his father's health, warding off those who would trouble him unnecessarily, and doing all he can to disseminate Juche Thought.[7]

Never is he shown simply enjoying himself. His clothes are simple and austere, usually a zip-up tunic and matching pants in a drab brown; unlike his father he never wears suits. Artists like to portray the youthful Jong Il in solitude, often at a site associated with the anti-Japanese struggle, or looking on with a wistful smile as his father greets adoring citizens.[8] The message: For Kim Jong Il so loved the Korean people that he gave them his only parent.

Still, this is rather thin stuff to be making a personality cult out of, and one can only wonder how the public would have responded to the Dear Leader's accession had the nuclear crisis of the early 1990s not fitted him out with his own myth of national rescue. (We will discuss the conflict with America in the following chapter.) Even now the regime evidently feels the need for the dead Parent Leader to remind the masses what "enormous luck" they enjoy in having his son around, and that they must venerate the General "no matter what wind may blow in the future."[9] They must also take good care of his health, making sure that he gets enough rest, etc.[10] The regime seems to have an endless supply of these remarkably topical-sounding quotes, only a few of which can be traced back to Kim Il Sung's collected works.[11] It would appear that for all the propaganda apparatus's hard work, the Dear Leader is still far from enjoying the popularity that his father did. This problem is certainly not unconnected with the appearance of the real-life Kim Jong Il, a short, homely and now wizened man given to wearing sunglasses—eyewear often associated with Yankee villains—even in indoor photo-ops. (His voice is not particularly pleasant either, judging from South Korean footage of the 2000 summit, though like his father's voice— and Hirohito's until Japan's surrender—it is not heard in public.) But the masses' perception of his father as the greater of the two men undoubtedly has more to do with the power of the national liberation myth and the higher living standard they enjoyed under his rule.

The Kim Jong Il regime has always enjoyed a higher degree of uncoerced mass support than the outside world is willing to recognize.

This is not to imply that they blame Kim Jong Il for the famine of the mid-1990s. The propaganda apparatus has done far too good a job of blaming this second "Arduous March" (Kim Il Sung having led partisans on the alleged original march of that name) on other factors. Typical is Pak Il-Myŏng's "Transition," which appeared in June 1999.[12] This is one of many short stories in which everything the Leader thinks, does and says is *meant* to be understood as a product of the writer's imagination, yet true to the essence of the great man. "Transition" opens with the Leader seated behind a desk in an undisclosed location.

They say time flows like a river, and indeed, a year had somehow already been borne past as if on a swift current. Soon it would dawn on a new year, Juche

86 (1998). The drizzle that had begun the day before showed signs of abating, only to turn into an untidy downpour. In the unseasonal rain the earth, which was usually frozen rock-solid at this time of year, now squelched underfoot. Having given on-the-spot guidance and inspections to the People's Army troops right up until the end of the year, the Great Ruler Kim Jong Il had a short while before returned to his desk and, without a moment's rest, set about reading the collectively-penned editorials that would be printed in the new year's party, military and youth newspapers.[13]

While Kim Il Sung was and still is associated in the arts with sunshine and blue skies, his son is often pictured in inclement weather, or standing on the seashore as waves crash against the rocks. In "Transition," too, he is introduced amidst references to mud and rain—a reminder that he faces even more challenging circumstances than his father did.

It had been a hard year. The continuation of the imperialists' political and economic blockade, and, on the world's stage, war and strife, starvation and extreme poverty, historically unprecedented oppression threatening all mankind—it had been a year in which these things had enveloped the earth like a black cloud.[14]

Note that blame for the republic's problems is placed on factors beyond Kim's control: the imperialist blockade and a worldwide increase in general misery. Significant is also the implication that things are worse in other countries. (The official media have always made much of the worst famines and natural disasters in Africa and elsewhere.)

Enter the Watson-like sidekick, a fixture of all stories of this kind. Kyŏng'u, a party official, has just returned from a fact-finding trip to the countryside. Knowing that the Dear Leader prizes honesty above all else, he reveals that while the state expects regions to supply their own fertilizer, "the actual results... fall far short of the plan."[15]

Kim Jong Il responds:

> "Long ago the Leader [i.e. Kim Il Sung] was already calling agriculture the foundation of the universe... But we have not farmed well in recent years, and we have failed to implement his teachings properly. To make matters worse, we have suffered damages from floods and drought, so that now the people are enduring difficulty because of the food problem. But still no one complains. Even while eating gruel they are steadfastly surmounting difficulties. They're worried they might otherwise cause me pain, you see. When I think how much the Leader wanted to give our people white rice and meat soup, I find it hard to bear..."
>
> "We have not properly taken on the work you gave us to do, General," Kyŏng'u said as he hung his head.

So a food shortage is admitted, if not a famine, and ascribed to a combination of natural disasters and the general failure to implement Kim Il Sung's teachings. Kyŏng'u's shamefacedness makes clear that the people have let the Leader down, not vice versa. The cadre then makes bitter reference to the *Schadenfreude* of western news agencies, which are predicting more difficult times for the DPRK.

Kim's reply:

"More difficult, eh... It's possible. But... I think that instead of becoming more difficult, the situation will gradually resolve, just as the spring melts the snow. This faith comes from what I have felt while traveling around the past year. Of course the country's economy is now in a very difficult state. But in the new year reform must take place in every part of the people's economy. Can it be done? I think there is no end to what can be done. No matter how difficult the economic situation is now, it is completely different from the situation after the war, when socialist construction had to be launched on a pile of ashes. Now we have the foundation of a self-supporting economy that the Leader laid down for us.... I think it all depends on the workers themselves.[16]

So Kim believes things will improve, *but maybe they won't.* Everything depends on the workers—he *thinks.* His father never sounded so uncertain. The reader is left wondering just what role the Dear Leader sees for himself on the economic front. The image of snow melting in springtime suggests that it is not a very active one. All the same, he offers a solution to the fertilizer shortage:

"Some cadres now think there can be no farming without fertilizer, but this is wrong. Did we ever complain about the lack of fertilizer after liberation? Even if you look at the international trend, it's toward farming with less fertilizer."

These words brought Kyŏng'u to his senses at once. Had he not been one of those cadres, complaining about fertilizer when he should have been looking for a way out of the difficulties?

"General, I thought wrongly."[17]

Granted, Kim Il Sung expressed himself on a comparably trite level, but it is one thing to call rainbow trout a tasty fish, and another to suggest, as Kim Jong Il does here, that his country should surmount the lack of something by using less of it. This is clearly a personality cult for straitened times.

Our hero then proposes a drive into the countryside, with himself at the wheel. Soon he spots an elderly woman walking by the side of the road.

"Someone coming back from the market would not be out alone this late. Judging from the difficulty she's having walking, it is clear that she has either come a very long way or is exhausted with hunger."

Kim Jong Il felt a pang in his breast. He was seeing in the grandmother the pain being endured by the people.[18]

In the most explicit indication of the extent of the food shortage, the writer describes her as "gaunt from loss of weight."[19] The General stops the sedan and offers to take her to her destination. Tales of one or the other Kim giving average citizens a ride are common in the Text, and the story plays out here in familiar fashion: the woman improbably fails to recognize who has picked her up, the cadre wrings his hands over her irreverence, and the Leader chuckles indulgently. As it turns out, the old woman has left her son's home to live with her daughter, so disgusted is she with him. A party secretary at a coal mine, he can think of no response to the mine's recent collapse than to brood in his office. She recounts the angry speech she made:

> Everyone talks about the Arduous March this, the Arduous March that, but how many people are really going through it? The only one is the General [Kim Jong Il] himself. Ask your conscience, am I talking hot air? You know from watching TV. Doesn't our General go up and down steep mountain paths without a moment's rest in order to visit with the People's Army troops? He's trying to keep watch over the Homeland, over all of us. And he always insists on eating just what the people are eating, maize rice and gruel.... Is it enough just to *talk* about taking care of him? We've got to dig a lot of coal, coal I tell you.[20]

Such talk is standard. In the Text soldiers and veterans routinely burst into tears at the memory of how their units had to feed the visiting General gruel or millet instead of white rice.[21] Artists and illustrators whip up guilt further by depicting Kim on especially arduous stations of his endless national tour: visiting military outposts during a storm or blizzard, or walking up to his trouser-clad knees in a canal.[22]

But while the regime emphasizes the hardship of Kim's life, it does not go so far as to depict him as ascetic, for that would imply a lack of Korean spontaneity. He is thus depicted as corpulent and cheerful, albeit not to the same degree of either quality as his father was and is still shown. He too indulges in the occasional cigarette.[23] The main visual sign of his self-sacrifice is his drab and unassuming dress. The famous gray parka, which he allegedly designed himself, is as common in the visual arts as in newspaper photographs.[24]

Just because Kim is exempted from criticism for the nation's difficulties does not mean that he is denied credit for its successes. The difference to the Kim Il Sung cult is that the General's leadership in non-military areas is presented mainly as a matter of inspiration by example. To return to the story we have been discussing, the Dear Leader neither visits the mine nor offers its party secretary any advice; much as economic problems pain him, the military comes first. And yet we learn at the end that the mine overcame the crisis when workers resolved to "fight for the General."[25] In similar fashion, athletes and entertainers who have done well overseas invariably ascribe their triumph, just as prominent Koreans once did under Hirohito, to the leader whose love gave them strength and fortitude.[26]

One might well expect this "military-first" leader to cut a more masculine figure than Kim Il Sung, but he never looks more feminine than in the official portrait of him in a general's uniform; the artist is clearly intent on counteracting the martial aspect of the clothes themselves. Though Kim is often referred

to as "Father General," reports of his visits to army bases focus on his fussy concern for the troops' health and comfort.
"[He] went round education rooms, bedrooms, mess halls and
other places to acquaint himself with everything from the hu-
midity of the bedrooms in the rainy season to the preparation
of side-dishes..."[27] He is also increasingly referred to as "our
parent," though the fixed epithet Parent Leader is evidently still
reserved for Kim Il Sung.[28] That is not all: on occasion he is
explicitly referred to as a mother, and in martial contexts at
that. The following excerpt, which is strikingly reminiscent of
the imagery of Japanese wartime propaganda, puts the cult of
the "military-first" leader in a nutshell.

> Held together not by a mere bond between a lead-
> er and his warriors but by the family tie between a
> mother and her children, who share the same blood
> and breath, Korea will prosper forever. Let the impe-
> rialist enemies come at us with their nuclear weap-
> ons, for there is no power on earth that can defeat our
> strength and love and the power of our belief, which
> thanks to the blood bond between mother and child
> create a fortress of single-heartedness. Our Great
> Mother, General Kim Jong Il![29]

An enormous sign held up in a recent parade, footage of which
was shown on the television news in 2009 whenever "The
Song of General Kim Jong Il" was played, bore the slogan,
"We Cannot Live Away From His Breast."[30]

This is no empty rhetoric; the masses are reminded with
increasing frequency that because the nation cannot survive

without the leader who constitutes both its heart and its head, they must be ready to die to defend him. As if the logic were not in itself reminiscent of fascist Japan, the regime makes increasingly bold use of the very same terms—such as "resolve to die" (kyŏlsa) and "human bombs" (yukt'an)—that were so common in imperial Japanese and colonial Korean propaganda during the Pacific War.[31] In the summer of 2009 the evening news periodically played a stirring anthem entitled "We Will Give Our Lives to Defend the Head of the Revolution." The text runs, "Ten million will become as guns and bombs... to give one's life for the General is a soldier's greatest honor."[32.]

Kim Jong Il does not appear in the accompanying footage in person, but only through the banner of the Supreme Commander—an ornate five-pointed star on a red background—which now features as often in the visual arts as the flag of the republic itself. Has the Leader grown too visibly close to death himself for his physical appearance to move others to die for him? Perhaps, but this is not as big a problem as one might think. It cannot be stressed often enough that like his father, Kim Jong Il serves as the living symbol of the homeland; in acclaiming his perfect Koreanness, the masses acclaim themselves. Not for nothing does the suicidal anthem revel in images of soldiers goose-stepping in unison, and enormous crowds in torch-lit processions. For the average man these are far more seductive images than even the most impressive face could be; through their collective adulation of the Great Mother the masses regain what the psychoanalyst Otto Fenichel once called the "oceanic feeling" of the omnipotent's parent's love.[33.]

The need to play up the hardship of the Dear Leader's life has so far prevented the official media from acknowledging any of his wives, let alone showing a family portrait comparable to the ones in which Kim Jong Il appeared as a small boy. This may explain the uncharacteristic subtlety and coy vagueness of the current campaign to glorify Kim Jong Ŭn, the second son of Kim Jong Il's third wife, who is evidently the next in line for the succession. From what we can gather from outside the country, this campaign is still in an early stage, consisting of little more than regular performances, singalongs and textual displays of a panegyric entitled *Palgŏrŭm* or "Stride." A wall poster photographed in September 2009 bears the lyrics of the song under a legend congratulating the masses on being blessed not just with the General, but with "the young General Kim Jong Ŭn" as well. The latter, whose title is written with a different Korean word for general (*taejang*) than the one applied to his father (*changgun*), is described as carrying on both the "bloodline of Man'gyŏngdae," i.e. of Kim Il Sung's birthplace, and "the bloodline of Mount Paektu," i.e. the birthplace of Kim Jong Il. This roundabout way of indicating his parentage seems to reflect the regime's sense of awkwardness in celebrating someone whose very existence was kept secret for so long. The song itself, with its puerile onomatopoeic refrain, adds nothing to our knowledge of the young man. An excerpt:

Tramp, tramp, tramp
The footsteps of our General Kim
Spreading the spirit of February

A wall poster, photographed by a Taiwanese tourist in September 2009, congratulates citizens on being "blessed" with "the young General Kim Jong Ŭn." Below the legend is the panegyric "Stride."

Tramp, tramp, tramping onwards

…..

Bringing us closer to a brilliant future

The lyric's references to February may be allusions to Kim
Jong Il's birth-month, but may also refer to exploits of the
"young General" himself. There is no point speculating further about a nascent personality cult which will likely have
emerged into much sharper relief by the time this book is
published. But the most important fact of the cult is already
clear enough from its martial imagery: Although the transition to a successor presents a unique opportunity to retire the
military-first policy without a loss of face, the regime does
not plan to avail itself of it. The next leader's image will be
more in the mold of Kim Jong Il than Kim Il Sung.

CHAPTER FIVE
FOREIGNERS

North Korea is often characterized as "solipsistic," but racial pride always requires constant awareness of an inferior other. To the North Koreans the other is not just America, as so many foreigners believe, but the entire outside world, for if the child race is uniquely pure, it follows that no non-Koreans are to be regarded as equals.

Friendly nations such as Laos are therefore presented almost exclusively as tributary states. Their main function in the Text is to be described as hosting Juche study conferences, sending eulogies to the Leader, congratulating the DPRK on important anniversaries, and so on. China remains a unique case inasmuch as the main news media describe it in favorable terms (albeit with virtually no coverage of Chinese life) without misrepresenting it as looking to Pyongyang for inspiration and guidance. Nor are visits from Chinese leaders and diplomats described, as all other visits from foreigners are, in terms of servile pilgrimages. Since the end of South Korea's munificent Sunshine Policy in 2008, the propaganda apparatus has devoted unprecedented space and time to celebrating the Beijing-Pyongyang alliance, even if the growing scale of Chinese investment in the DPRK remains a taboo topic.

But no amount of economic and military aid can earn a foreign country the sort of good will that extends to parts of the Text intended exclusively for domestic consumption. While Chinese visitors to the war museum in Pyongyang are shown exhibits acknowledging their country's enormous sacrifice, locals are taken on another route where they see and hear no mention of it. A similar approach marks treatment of the DPRK's neighbor to the north-east. Visits from Russian delegations and military choruses enjoy pride of place on the nightly news, while in less prominent sources of propaganda the USSR, for all its decades of patronage, is looked back on with contempt. Khrushchev is denounced as a "traitor," one of the "fake communists" who betrayed world socialism.[1] In a historical novel, Kim Il Sung chuckles about how he learned Soviet secrets by getting Brezhnev drunk.[2] There are frequent (and for the foreign reader unsettling) sneers about how the USSR collapsed "without firing a shot."[3]

Typical of the disdain shown even to the friendliest foreigners is a panoramic painting of a procession of exultant visitors to 1989's Pyongyang World Youth Games.[4] Whatever direction they happen to be looking in, their faces are all partly obscured by a sinister shadow. A fat Caucasian woman wears a low-cut blouse, while a few African women sport what appear to be halter-tops: even in today's DPRK such clothing is considered indecent. Here and there, unsavory-looking men show long sideburns and denim, more signs of Western decadence. The only well-groomed and attractive person in view, and the only one whose face is evenly lit, is the Korean guide—a girl, naturally—who leads the way in traditional dress. There are no Koreans in the procession proper; the pure race must be kept apart.[5] On the rare occasions in the Text when foreigners and locals meet, the former employ highly respectful, sometimes obsequious Korean, while the latter respond informally as if to subordinates.[6] Real fraternity between the pure and the impure is impossible; the DPRK's so-called Friendship Museum contains only gifts given by foreigners—"offered up," as the Text always puts it—to the Leaders.[7]

While the Text strongly implies that all foreigners are inferior, and occasionally criticizes the Jews' influence on world affairs, it subjects only the Japanese and Americans to routine vituperation.[†] As might be expected, the "Japs" (*oenom*) feature mainly in accounts of the colonial era. In contrast to Soviet depictions of the Germans in World War II, the Text does not distinguish between colonial-era Japanese according to class; all are inherently rapacious. It follows that they have no right to humane treatment. In this scene from a classic novel of the 1950s, one of Kim Il Sung's guerillas exacts retribution on an unarmed prisoner.

[†] The Jews' baleful influence on American politics is mentioned in *Ryŏksa ŭi taeha*, 226, *Ch'ongdae*, 262, while in *Yŏngsaeng*, 253, Kim Il Sung tells Jimmy Carter (whose reaction is not given) that the Jews are treacherous.

Kŭmchŏl could feel his bitter heart begin to open, the heart that could only open at the sight of Japs' blood.... The Jap's neck glistened greasily like a pig's. When Kŭmchŏl saw it the fire in his breast raged intensely.... He yanked the bastard up by the neck and dragged him out of the box, where he fell down again. Seeing he had pissed on the papers in the box from fear, Kŭmchŏl spat on his pale mug.... Unable to speak, the Jap bowed his head and pressed his hands together, pleading soundlessly for mercy.

"Son of a bitch! So you don't want to die?".... Kŭmchŏl wanted to cut the swine's neck open with his own hands."[8]

Sensing what is in store for him, the captive tries to run away, but the Korean catches up to him and deals his skull a furious kick. "The eyeballs sprang out of their sockets as the skull splattered against the barrack wall."[9]

In recent years, however, individual Japanese women have occasionally been portrayed as sympathetic to the Korean people or as admirers of the Dear Leader. A recent example is the serial film *The Country I Saw* (Nae ga pon nara, 2009), which depicts a female Japanese professor who is impressed by the military-first regime's string of victories over the United States.[10]

Needless to say, far more time and resources are spent vilifying the US than Japan. The following is a summary of the relevant anti-American myths.

Throughout its disgraceful history the United States has wrought misery on peace-loving people the world over.

After wiping out their continent's indigenous population and enslaving millions of Africans, the Yankees turned their attention to Korea, dispatching a gunship in 1866 to bully the proud nation into opening its markets. To the Yankees' surprise the Koreans refused to yield; none other than the Parent Leader's great-grandfather Kim Ung'u organized farmers into an attack force that sent the USS Sherman to the bottom of the Taedong River. Furious at this setback, the Yankees set about subverting the peninsula from within. Working first with landowners, then with the Japanese colonial administration, missionaries prowled the peninsula in search of converts for Christian churches, all the while committing unspeakable outrages against helpless children.

In 1945, while Kim Il Sung was busy routing the Japanese, the Yankees took advantage of the confusion to occupy the southern part of the peninsula, where they massacred democratic forces and installed a puppet government under "president" Syngman Rhee. On June 25, 1950 the Yankees and their lackeys launched a surprise attack on the DPRK, but the heroic People's Army drove them back. In desperation the Yankees resorted to the indiscriminate bombing of civilian targets, but still the Korean people refused to yield, and finally, on July 27 1953, the United States was forced to sign an abject surrender.

It was the first in a long string of Yankee defeats. In 1968 an American spy ship ventured brazenly into DPRK waters; it was captured at once and its crew held until the US issued a servile apology. A year later an American spy plane was shot down over Korean territory, but for all Washington's saber-rattling, which included the threat of nuclear attack, it ultimately did nothing. In 1976 People's Army soldiers at the DMZ were ambushed by

Missionaries in colonial Korea murder a child by injection; the legend calls for "revenge against the Yankee vampires." This poster appeared in 1999, when the US was the largest foreign aid donor to the DPRK.

axe-wielding Yankee troops; the Koreans wrested the axes from their attackers and killed two of them. Again Washington's bark proved worse than its bite.

The DPRK joined the Nuclear Non-Proliferation Treaty in 1985, but refused to allow inspections of its peaceful atomic program until the Yankees withdrew their nuclear weapons from south Korea—which they soon did. When the UN inspections of the DPRK's facilities ended without incident, the Americans incited impure elements inside the UN to demand inspections of additional sites. Naturally the DPRK refused to allow the enemy to lay bare one military secret after the other. Washington then announced that it would resume "Team Spirit" war rehearsals with south Korean soldiers.

In response the Dear Leader placed the DPRK on a war alert in March 1993, throwing the Yankees into a panic. Weeks later he struck a second blow by announcing that Korea would withdraw from the NPT. The Yankees promptly waved the white flag, promising the Leader's diplomatic warriors that they would cease their provocations and even provide the DPRK with light-water reactors. President Clinton personally affirmed his commitment to the treaty in a letter offered up to the Dear Leader. But despite their humiliating defeat the Americans continued scheming against Korean-style socialism.

In 2002 their new president Bush reverted to America's traditional strategy of threats and provocations, calling Korea part of an "axis of evil." The Dear Leader responded to this hard-line policy with a "super hard-line" policy of his own, successfully testing a nuclear deterrent in 2006. With this brilliant triumph Korea joined the world's most elite club, the club of nuclear powers. Again the Americans raged—and again they came crawling back to the negotiation table. In 2009 Clinton himself *came to North Korea to apologize for the illegal activities of two American journalists. The DPRK's military first policy has so intimidated the Yankees that even in south Korea they are lying low. The day is nigh when these jackals in human form—now as always the sole obstacle to national unification—will be driven from the peninsula for good.*[11]

Like the "Japs," the Yankees are condemned as an inherently evil race that can never change, a race with which Koreans must *forever* be on hostile terms. Readers should therefore not be misled by the Marxist jargon so common in the KCNA's English-language rhetoric. In propaganda meant only for the domestic audience, the terms "US imperialism" (mije) and "America" (miguk) are used interchangeably, and Americans referred to routinely as "nom" or bastards.[12] In a recent picture printed in the monthly art magazine, a child with a toy machine gun stands before a battered snowman. The caption reads, "The American bastard I killed."[13] The DPRK's dictionaries and schoolbooks encourage citizens to

speak of Yankees as having "muzzles," "snouts" and "paws"; as "croaking" instead of "dying," and so on.[14]

As in colonial Korea, propagandists are fond of demonizing missionaries, the better to combine an anti-American and an anti-Christian message.[15] Christianity is dismissed as a mere tool of infiltration and subversion; one recent poster shows a copy of the Bible with the Statue of Liberty on its cover.[16] The following depiction of a missionary family comes from the hugely popular novella *Jackals* (Sŭngnyangi, 1951), in which a Korean child is murdered by a mysterious injection of germs. (The crime is now treated as historical fact.)[†] The writer makes clear that the Americans' evil can be "read" in their big noses, large breasts and sunken eyes.

> The old jackal's spade-shaped eagle's nose hung villainously over his upper lip, while the vixen's teats jutted out like the stomach of a snake that has just swallowed a demon, and the slippery wolf-cub gleamed with poison like the head of a venomous snake that has just swallowed its skin. Their six sunken eyes seemed... like open graves constantly waiting for corpses.[17]

As might be expected, the Korean War occupies a central place in anti-American propaganda, but the Text dwells less on the US Air Force's extensive bombing campaign (which is hard to reconcile with the myth of a protective Leader) than on village massacres and other isolated outrages. The massacre of tens of thousands of civilians in Sinch'ŏn in October 1950 (which was actually perpetrated by Korean rightists) is held up as the Yankees' most heinous crime.[‡] The nightly news regularly shows groups being led through the museum in the

[†] In 2002 I visited a re-settlement facility for refugees near Seoul, where I was eyed with open hostility. When I finally managed to engage a teenager in conversation, she said, "Americans did bad things in Korea." When I asked her to elaborate, she told me haltingly about missionaries in the colonial era who killed a child for—she put her head to one side—was it taking fruit from their orchard? *Ch'ŏllima*, inside back cover, May 1999.

[‡] The South Korean writer Hwang Sŏk-yŏng's novel *Sonnim* (*The Guest*, 2001), based on eye-witness accounts of the massacre, inspired an MBC television documentary in 2002, which confirmed Hwang's assertion that the killings had taken place just before the arrival of American troops.

village by ever-indignant female guides. A typical illustration of the massacre shows US soldiers menacing captured Korean women. As is common with Yankee villains, the commanding officer has a white neck, Caucasian features and a dark-skinned face; presumably such depictions are meant to convey the contaminated nature of American racial stock to the domestic viewer without insulting the DPRK's African allies.[18] The Text does its best to celebrate the truce of July 27,

A poster commemorating the Sinch'ŏn massacre of October 1950 "Let us not forget the grudge over Sinch'ŏn!"

Above: The iconic photograph of the USS Pueblo crew after their capture in 1968. Below: The poster reads: "If the US imperial-ist indiscriminately lash out, they will not be able to escape the fate off the USS Pueblo!"

1953 as a crushing defeat for the Americans, but incessant calls to avenge their crimes reflect a painful awareness that the enemy got off far too easily.[19]

Gloating over the capture of the USS Pueblo in 1968 is more truly felt. History books treat it as the shining highlight of North Korea's long-running confrontation with the United States. The photograph of the hapless crew with their hands in the air is the single most iconic image of the enemy; there are even postage stamps of it. The short story *Snowstorm in Pyongyang* (P'yŏngyang ŭi nunbora, 2000) contrasts the Pueblo prisoners' filth and depravity with the purity of the child race. Frequent showers do nothing to alleviate the Yankees' nauseating stench, so that a KPA soldier finally refuses to go on cutting their hair.[20] In a half-revolted, half-jeering tone, the narrator tells the scandalous back stories of the captured "bastards." One crewmember, it is claimed, felt so disillusioned by the incestuous goings on in his family that he "began sleeping with whatever women came his way. Tiring of that, he became gay."[21]

The Text regards homosexuality as a characteristically American "perversion." Here one of the Pueblo's crew pleads for the right to indulge it in captivity.

"Captain, sir, homosexuality is how I fulfill myself as a person. Since it does no harm to your esteemed government or esteemed nation, it is unfair for Jonathan and me to be prevented from doing something that is part of our private life."

[The North Korean soldier responds,] "This is the territory of our republic, where people enjoy lives befitting human beings. On this soil none of that sort of activity will be tolerated."[22]

The US government having apologized for spying, the prisoners are led off. At the same time a snowstorm rages, "as if intent on sweeping the country clean of all the filthy ugly revolting traces" left behind by the Yankees.[23]

Let us turn now to the Text's treatment of the ongoing nuclear dispute. Here too the contrast to Soviet propaganda is stark. Where Moscow always professed a respect for international law, the North Koreans reject the notion that a pure race should be bound by the dictates of an impure world. The Text thus cheerfully admits that the DPRK joined the Non-Proliferation Treaty in 1985 only to "use" it for the country's own ends, whereupon it "ignored" or "scorned" the treaty's stipulations.[24] The "diplomatic warriors" of the DPRK's Foreign Ministry roam the world at will, barging into the offices of frightened officials to make blunt, rude demands. In the following passage from one of the most highly celebrated novels of 1997, Deputy Foreign Minister Mun Sŏn-gyu (a thinly disguised version of Kang Sŏk-chu, who held the title at the time) calls on Hans Blix in Vienna. [25]

> Mun sat down and, before the IAEA Director General could open his mouth, said in English, "I have come to rigorously protest the agency's discriminatory pressure on us."
>
> Hans Blix was stunned. They had not even exchanged greetings according to diplomatic custom. This was almost unheard of in international relations.

But before he could find words to express himself, Mun protested again.

"How could the agency send us such an unfair agreement? And why do you keep applying pressure on us to sign it?"

"Well, hold on there...this is so sudden...it's a little...." Blix seemed to be thinking rapidly. He needed to figure out how best to respond to Mun's straightforward attack [....]

Mun continued in the same unyielding tone. "Last year the head of our treaty office gave a detailed clarification of our position [....] So why did the agency send us a discriminatory agreement to sign? Does it think we are idiots, ignorant of international rules and indifferent to our own dignity?"

The discriminatory document in question was one applicable to countries that had not entered the Non-Proliferation Treaty and was aimed at ensuring the regulation of atomic facilities and equipment. Signatories to the NPT, on the other hand, were subjected only to inspection of atomic material, which is why Mun pressed this point so firmly.[26]

So although the DPRK had hitherto "ignored" the NPT's stipulations, Mun wants it treated like a member in good standing. Perhaps aware of the shamelessness of his own demand, he does not appear genuinely angry. Instead he is amusing himself by bullying Blix. Readers are clearly meant to be amused too:

Squirming, Blix raised both his hands. "That was just a mistake…. A mistake! It was an error on the part of our officials. I wasn't even aware of it until your esteemed country protested. Didn't I even send a letter of apology, albeit a belated one, to your esteemed country? Isn't that enough?"

"No, it's not enough."

At Mun's hard and clipped response Blix stretched out his arms again. "But what else do you need? For heaven's sake, what other pledge do you need?"[27]

Mun replies that America's nuclear weapons must be withdrawn from South Korea at once. Blix stammers out his acquiescence:

"Ah, ah, I understand. Very good. I am very grateful to your esteemed country's government for making its position known with such honesty…. Are all your esteemed country's diplomats so direct?"

"Why," Mun retorted, "you don't like that?"

"N-no. On the contrary. Honest and very clear… it's very good. But… I wonder how best to call such a diplomacy…."

Mun laughed out loud.[28]

The Text has a term for it: "attack diplomacy."[29] Attributed to Kim Jong Il's own desire to see his Foreign Ministry behaving "aggressively and combatively," it is by no means reserved for America and its lackeys.[30] One "diplomatic warrior" tells Russia that it "should not impudently stick its nose into another country's affairs."[31] On the other hand, the regime is mindful enough of its relationship with Beijing not to revile (at least not in print) the entire United Nations, but only the "impure elements" inside it that allegedly do America's bidding.

Needless to say, the race-oriented Text makes little distinction between political factions in Washington; Democrats and Republicans, "doves" and "hawks" are all said to be bent on destroying the DPRK.[32] (Barack Obama's accession to the US presidency in 2009 led to no reduction or softening of anti-American propaganda.) Nor can the Text acknowledge that America might refrain from a military attack in order to save Korean lives. The pure and the impure can have no common interests. Still less can the Text entertain the notion that the impure might defy their instincts. "Just as a jackal cannot become a lamb," runs a maxim known in minor variations to every North Korean, "the US imperialists cannot change their rapacious nature."[33]

This leaves the Text with no way to interpret America's readiness to negotiate except as a "kneeling down" or "waving of the white flag" in the face of Pyongyang's terrifying strength and unity.[34] President Clinton's letter promising "His Excellency Kim Jong Il" full compliance with the terms of the Agreed Framework appears in the official encyclopedia as a trophy of the "shining victory" of 1994.[35] The enemy's failures of nerve are portrayed as characteristic not only of the US, but of non-Asian foreigners in general. (I have already referred to the mockery of the USSR's "surrender.") In this passage from a propaganda novel, which is typical of the DPRK's sneaking respect for Hirohito's war machine, the Dear Leader recalls how Britain was taken down a peg or two during the Pacific War.

> In his 1943 attack on Singapore, General Tomoyuki Yamashita, "the Tiger of Asia," demanded the allies' unconditional surrender, requesting that General Archibald Percival Wavell answer either "yes" or "no".... Wavell at last spat out the word "yes" and hung his head. Since then use of he word "yes" in negotiations is regarded in the West as a symbol of subjugation and shame. But history has repeatedly forced the vanquished to say this humiliating word. At the Korean War truce talks the UN Commander Clarke had no choice but to answer "yes" to our demand that he surrender. In later years, after the Pueblo incident and the downing of the E-121 plane, the enemies bayed for war like madmen, but ultimately when we asked the stern question, "Will it be war?" they had no choice but to answer "no." And when we said, "Will it be talks?" they had no choice but to answer "yes.".... Our people, our invincible People's Army is asking, so answer them! No need for a long answer. One word will do. War? "No." Talks? "Yes."
>
> Kim Jong Il smiled....[36]

The Text thus treats the negotiations leading up to the Agreed Framework of 1994 as having taken place between a victorious DPRK and a vanquished USA.[37] The content of these and all other negotiations is overlooked, the regime being unable to admit that it would so much as listen to requests for concessions. Instead readers are treated to peripheral dialogues like this:

> America had no choice but to grovel.
>
> Gallucci: "We respect you. The future peace not only of the Korean peninsula but also of Asia, the Pacific Region, depends on us, on the US and [North] Korea."
>
> Mun: "Whose words are those? Yours?"
>
> Gallucci. "The words of the White House."
>
> Mun: "That amounts to saying that we're a superpower too."
>
> Gallucci: "That's right, you're a superpower. A superpower like America!"
>
> Now Korea was on an equal footing with the United States, the world's only superpower. Asia's small country Korea, which had once lost its luster on the world map....[38]

As I mentioned in the historical part of this book, the assertion that America signed the Agreed Framework out of fear creates a logical inconsistency in the Text. On the one hand, the Clinton administration's claims that the DPRK was developing a nuclear arsenal are condemned as outrageous lies, while on the other hand heavy hints are dropped that a bomb *already* existed at the time. In a novel set in 1993 (and published in 2000), Kim Jong Il vows he will retaliate against any nuclear attack by turning America, in a single day, into "a sea of fire."[39]

Of course, many in the West will shrug this off as bravado masking a deep fear of American attack. How could the DPRK not be afraid, after what it endured in the Korean War? But in the early 1960s, East Bloc diplomats registered their worry that the North Koreans were too *dismissive* of the American threat, even talking of another attempt at liberating the South, despite the nuclear weapons stationed there at the time.[40] And that was before the DPRK embarked on its unbroken string of successful provocations of the superpower, from the USS Pueblo capture in 1968 to its detainment and show-trial of two American journalists in 2009. Suffice to say that there is no trace of fear of any adversary in the Text. (One is struck by the contrast to anti-American propaganda in East Germany during the 1980s, which constantly raised the specter of nuclear war.) On the contrary, the child race is depicted as itching for a "holy war" or *sŏngjŏn*—once a common term in Pacific War propaganda— in which to kill Yankees and reunite the motherland.[41] "No matter how the Americans threaten us with their foolish war plans," Kim Jong Il chuckles in a novel set in 1998, "we are not frightened in the least."[42] Clinton and his men, meanwhile, express grudging respect for the "iron man" of Pyongyang and terror of the DPRK's long-range missiles, which are faster and more accurate than America's own.[43]

The disconnect between Washington's bark and its bite is contrasted with North Korean resolve. "If we say we do something, we do it," a gargantuan KPA soldier shouts in one poster as he slams his fist down on the continental USA. "We don't utter empty words!"[44] Other posters show wish-fulfilling images of fighter planes or missiles destroying the US Capitol.[45] Yankee soldiers are depicted as spindly, insect-like creatures, dwarfed by enormous Korean fists, hoisted effortlessly on bayonets, or squashed under missiles.[46] Even mathematics textbooks reinforce the impression of a hopelessly outclassed foe: "Three People's Army soldiers

rubbed out thirty American bastards. What was the ratio of the soldiers who fought?" etc.[47] Also common are calls to "sweep" the Yankees from the peninsula like so much dirt.[48]

The myth of an America quaking in constant terror of the DPRK has enabled the regime to explain away food aid shipments, which began arriving in the mid-1990s, in terms of reparations.[49] The Yankees are also depicted (and not without a basis in truth) as paying in grain for the right to undertake fruitless inspections of suspected nuclear sites.[50]

> "Excellency! We in the (US) Department of Defense hope to have your military facility at Kŭmch'angni revealed to us, no matter what it takes. Please tell us the price of viewing it."
>
> Pong Myŏng-ju looked down on Dunne with a dignified smile. "Due to your economic blockade and natural disasters we are now going through...difficulties. Looking at things from a humanitarian aspect, and in view of the consequences of our conflict with you, we regard 700 thousand tons of grain as appropriate."[51]

This propaganda line is the reason why North Korean citizens are permitted to use aid sacks, including those emblazoned with the US flag, as carry-alls.

For most of the 1990s, the regime's desire to pose as both an invincible superpower *and* an aggrieved victim of American slander forced the Text into an almost comical vagueness. The masses were told only that Washington had trumped up "some so-called nuclear problem," and so on. Things became less complicated after Pyongyang explicitly acknowledged the existence of a "deterrent to nuclear war"

in 2003. Since the testing of this deterrent in October 2006—
followed by another American "surrender," i.e. a return to
talks—less attention has been devoted to the back-story of the
nuclear saga, which, quite apart from its logical holes, now
seems rather dull in comparison.

Since 2006 the propaganda apparatus has engaged in all-out
acclamation of the "military-first" policy that made the DPRK
a nuclear power. (Only the Great Leader's liberation of the
peninsula now occupies a more important place in the national
history.) The masses are to believe that America now has even
greater respect and fear of its adversary, a message unwittingly
confirmed by the superpower's recent peace overtures, such as
the New York Philharmonic's visit to the DPRK in February
2008. When former president Bill Clinton flew to Pyongyang in
August 2009 to win the release of two detained US journalists,
the official media made much of the deference and contrition
shown to the Great Ruler by his erstwhile foe. (It was also
claimed, though the US State Department denied it, that Clinton
had conveyed an oral message from President Obama.)[52] The
Korean bomb is even said to have intimidated the Yankees into
assuming a lower profile in their colony to the south. On theater
stages, clowns with noses enlarged by putty play GI's bumbling
around amidst the increasingly rebellious South Koreans. In a
recent comic strip, US military officers ask a passing local to
take their picture. Promising the perfect backdrop, he leads
them to the UN cemetery.[53]

But America is too important a scapegoat for the regime
ever to claim to have defeated it once and for all. To do so would
be to raise public expectations of a drastic improvement in living
standards, the immediate reunification of the peninsula, and
everything else that Washington is now accused of preventing.

The enemy must therefore always be shown reneging on the terms of its latest surrender.[54] Lest anyone think that nuclear talks might lead to a different relationship with the US, Kim Jong Il himself is quoted as saying, "The Yankees are the eternal enemies of our masses; we cannot live under the same sky with them."[55] A common way to whip up anger during periods of lesser tension is to demand vengeance for America's historical crimes against the race.[56]

The poem "To Grow Up Quickly, Quickly," (2004) aims to instill this thirst for revenge in children by reminding them of the alleged American massacre at Sinch'ŏn during the Korean War:

> How bitter [General Kim Jong Il] must have felt
> To remain so long
> Before the grave of the 102 children
> Clenching his fists in silence.
>
> The Father General must have come
> To Sinch'ŏn, where all children my age died
> To make sure that in this land,
> There would never be another bloody Sinch'ŏn...
>
> So, taking that resolve to my own heart,
> I am going to join the army;
> I will take two guns, three guns
> And shoot down all the American bastards
> Ah, to grow up quickly
> To grow up quickly, quickly...[57]

There is much talk of this "blood reckoning" that the nation's elders expect the younger generation to execute. "Our masses have already imposed a death sentence on US imperialism," a literary journal intoned in 2006. "We will certainly carry it out."[58]

Yet the rhetoric usually stops just short of demanding an offensive invasion of the South. The standard message can be reduced to the following nutshell: We will destroy the Yankees and their lackeys, re-uniting the motherland in the process, if they dare attack or provoke us.[59] But the regime's notion of what constitutes an act of war against it—economic sanctions, attempts to inspect its ships, etc—grows ever broader. Posters now threaten America and Japan with a devastating reprisal if they so much as insult the republic. One caption: "We will reckon decisively with anyone, anywhere who meddles with our self-respect."[60] There is no discounting the possibility that the armed forces receive an even more bellicose form of the Text than the population at large.

Ideologies that divide a virtuous in-group from an evil outside world always do an excellent job of unifying the in-group. "Hatred is probably the most spontaneous and common sentiment," Jacques Ellul wrote. "Propaganda of agitation succeeds each time it designates someone as the source of all misery, provided he is not too powerful."[61] The Americans are still vilified in precisely those terms, as they never were in Soviet propaganda. The line, "The Yankees are the source of all our masses' misery and suffering" is belabored especially often in June and July, which, due to the anniversaries of the war's beginning and end, are to anti-US invective what February, March and April are for the Kim cults.[62]

The anti-American short story
"Jackals" (1951) was simultaneously republished in three
magazines in August 2003,
just as the Six Party Talks were
due to begin. Above, the story's
missionary-villain in one of
the accompanying illustrations.

To Bruce Cumings and other left-leaning observers, these expressions of anti-Americanism reflect a more or less popular and untutored anger at US outrages in the Korean War. I happen to agree with Cumings that the bombing of the DPRK (which included plentiful use of napalm) was carried out with enough indifference to the lives of civilians to constitute a war crime. Let us bear in mind, however, that a) no other bombed-out country has borne a grudge with such fervor for so long, b) that anti-American propaganda was hardly less intense before the Korean War than after it and c) that *Jackals* (1951), the Text's main anti-American tale, is not about the war but about missionary child-killers: a tale, in other words, with one obvious root in nineteenth-century peasant rumor and another in fascist Japan's anti-Christianity campaign.

It is no coincidence that a poster illustrating that story's central crime—the caption: "100,000 times revenge on the Yankee vampires"—appeared in 1999, when North Korea was the Clinton administration's main aid-recipient in Asia.[63] Nor was it by accident that *Jackals* was simultaneously republished, complete with racist caricatures, in three magazines in August 2003, just before and during the first round of the six-party talks.[64] Ever since Kim Jong Il proclaimed his "military-first" government, effectively shaking off responsibility for the country's economic ruin, declines in real-world tension between Pyongyang and Washington have seen an intensification of anti-Americanism, not a lessening of it. Only one conclusion is possible: The regime is worried that the masses might cease to perceive the US as an enemy, thus leaving it with no way to justify its rule—or even to justify the existence of the DPRK as a separate state.

CHAPTER SIX
THE YANKEE COLONY

The regime's discussion of South Korea—or "south Korea" as its English-language organs prefer to call it—has always differed starkly from the *Sozialkritik* that East Germany once brought to bear on its rival. Faced with a porous border to West Berlin and constant infiltration by Western television and radio broadcasts, the GDR had no choice but to concede the outward signs of affluence and freedom in the Federal

Republic. Propaganda sought to persuade the East German people that the glittering exterior masked "contradictions" in the capitalist system that doomed it to ruin. As the West's economy pulled further ahead, the communists found it ever harder to get this message across; the rest is history. Kim Il Sung, in contrast, had little problem keeping heterodox influences out of his domain. By the mid-1960s he had sealed his citizens off even from the socialist bloc. As a result his propaganda apparatus was free to depict South Korea as the impoverished antipode to the North's "paradise on earth": a "living hell" where children rummaged for food in trash heaps while American soldiers shot at them for target practice.[1]

The rapid deterioration of the information cordon in the latter 1990s forced Kim Il Sung's successor to drop that propaganda line, and admit that South Koreans had come to enjoy a higher standard of living than their brethren in the DPRK. If the masses took this revelation in stride, as they appear to have done, it was because the "Yankee colony" had always been condemned more on nationalist and moralist than on Marxist-Leninist grounds.

After the North-South summit in June 2000, the KCNA and the *Rodong Sinmun* newspaper cut back on their coverage of the South and refrained completely from direct attacks on Kim Dae Jung, thus conveying the impression of a Sunshine-induced thaw in relations. There were also carefully worded editorials that welcomed North-South "exchanges" while stopping short of recognizing the South's right to exist. Anti-ROK propaganda in these high-profile sources was largely reduced to: the ironic use of quotation marks when referring to the country's official name ("Han'guk") and institutions ("government," "national assembly," etc); the one-sided if sober reporting of bad news from the South (diseases, accidents, etc) and the histrionic condemnation of its conservative opposition.

Meanwhile a hard-line anti-South message continued to be spread by schoolbooks, novels, oral propaganda, party lecture materials, and other forms of propaganda that the outside world was rightly expected to overlook.

A brief summary of the myth of the "Yankee colony":

In 1945, just after the Great Leader Kim Il Sung had defeated the Japanese, the Yankees took advantage of the temporary chaos to occupy the southern half of the peninsula. Setting up a puppet regime in Seoul under the traitor Syngman Rhee, they brutally crushed the people's councils that had sprung up across the south—killing tens of thousands of people on Cheju Island alone—and reinstated pro-Japanese collaborators to positions of power and influence. Rejecting the Great Leader's call for a pan-Korean election, Rhee proclaimed the "Republic of Korea" in 1948.

In June 25, 1950 the Yankees and their stooges launched a surprise attack on the DPRK, but were repelled, and finally surrendered on July 27, 1953. Thwarted in their scheme to destroy Korean socialism, the Yankees set about exploiting their puppet state with renewed vengeance, all the while waiting for another opportunity to attack the DPRK. For decades the southern brethren were forced to live in abject poverty, suffering the brutal oppression of the puppet dictatorship and enduring the crimes and outrages committed by rampaging US troops. In 1980 the Yankees and the Chun Doo Hwan clique colluded in the massacre of young demonstrators in Kwangju, but the forces of freedom and democracy would not be silenced. Again and again they took to the streets, finally forcing the "Republic of Korea," in desperation, to claim that military rule had ended.

A civilian "government" was "elected," but behind the façade of "democracy" the Yankees continued pulling the strings. Fortunately the military-first policy of General Kim Jong Il has so frightened and confounded the Yankees that they dare not oppress their colony as heavy-handedly as before. In 2000 the puppet "government" had no choice but to yield to the southern masses' demands for inter-Korean cooperation. At a meeting that year in Pyongyang the Dear Leader had the south Korean "president" sign an agreement pledging to pursue unification without American intervention. In the following years inter-Korean economic cooperation flourished, leading to a rapid improvement in the quality of life in the Yankee colony. The southern masses are acutely aware that were it not for the DPRK's military-first policy, the Yankees would long since have plunged them into another ruinous war. They owe their material comfort to the self-sacrifice not only of the Dear Leader, but of all the heroic citizens of the DPRK. To be sure, this material comfort is but paltry compensation for the Yankee's defiling presence. The south Koreans' most fervent wish, now as before, is to live in a free and united nation under the Dear Leader's rule. Unfortunately the drive for unification suffered a setback in 2008, when the traitor Lee Myung Bak took over as the new "president" of the puppet state, vowing to turn back the clock on inter-Korean cooperation...[2]

Because the ROK is now condemned almost exclusively on ethnocentric and moralistic grounds, the Text is free not only to concede the rival state's economic affluence *but even to exaggerate it*, the evident aim being to inoculate the masses against future revelations. No amount of wealth, the message runs, can still the southern brethren's yearning for freedom and purification. The typical "south Korean" in the visual arts is thus no longer a starving child on a junk heap but a handsome man in a suit waving the so-called unification flag (the peninsula in blue against a white background) or a fashionably dressed college girl thrilled by the projected image of Kim Jong Il's signature.[3] The novel *Encounter* (Mannam, 2001) introduces readers to a young journalist in Seoul who can somehow afford both a flashy car and a house in the city center. His free time is spent wandering with his girlfriend "from cinema to video room and theater, zoo, botanical gardens, Mount Chiri and Mount Sŏrak, discotheque and beach."[4]

Of course, this superficial affluence masks a world of ethnic contaminations. In contrast to the DPRK, where the people are "as pure as the water they drink," the South is polluted in every sense. In *Encounter* a south Korean girl says:

The regime attributes the influx of heterodox culture to a US scheme to destabilize the country; in fact, the most popular DVDs and videos in the DPRK are of South Korean origin.

> 'Han'guk' *[the South Korean word for Korea—BRM]* is making its world debut as the flashiest of American colonies, so much so that the Americans tout it as a model. But look under the silk encasing, and you see the body of what has degenerated to a foul whore of America. Here and there covered in bruises from where it has been kicked black and blue by the American soldiers' boots, or decaying from where the American

sewage has seeped in. And out of all of that has come
a rotten "president," a rotten "government," rotten
media…. [I]t turns the stomach just to imagine it.[5]

Plenty of attention is devoted to the dangers of life in the South.
The following excerpt from the novel *Ah, Motherland* (*A, choguk*,
2004) refers to South Korea under Kim Dae Jung's rule.

Here in this accident-filled "republic," with its traffic
accidents and collapsing buildings, this country that
likes putting its former presidents in prison, the media
does not enlighten people about the world so much
as keep them in the dark…. Do you know how many
cars are stolen every year? The place is full of thieves.
120 people disappear every day, everywhere there are
assaults, violent gangs, the subway is a hell-way…. You
know the only thing this South Korea leads the world
in? In indictments and reports to the police it's number
one. It's five, ten times the level of other countries, so
mightn't one just as well say that the whole country
consists of snitches and police detectives? Where else
can one find such a disgraceful state of affairs?[6]

Just what America seeks to achieve in its colony is left unclear,
as is the extent and nature of its control. The Text wants to
present a colony groaning under the Yankee yoke, but it also
wants to mock the occupying power's failure to control its
subjects. It indulges the latter urge more often; nothing is more
contemptible to the North Korean worldview than weakness.
South Korea's rulers (including the dictator Park Chung Hee)
are more likely to be shown scraping obsequiously before their

foreign masters than cracking down on basic freedoms. The lowest ranking representatives of the colonial power come in for the brunt of vilification. Straw-haired, beak-nosed GI's, often in dark glasses or Military Police helmets, are shown harassing women on darkened streets or committing outrages against local children: running them over for a laugh, say, or "adopting" them for use as house-slaves.[7] These are rather tame allegations compared to propaganda disseminated before the mid-1990s. The public's growing awareness of the real South Korea has made it impossible for the Text to keep claiming (for example) that the Yankees use children for shooting practice. One is to believe that the "military-first" policy has frightened the Americans into behaving better. Every week the *Rodong sinmun* quotes half-identified South Koreans ("a Mr. Kim in Seoul," "a professor in Busan") who express their gratitude to the Dear Leader for his "super-hardline" stance.[8]

Especially interesting are North Korea's efforts to discredit President Kim Dae Jung, the architect of the accomodationist Sunshine Policy. In real life a left-wing nationalist sympathetic to Pyongyang, he is depicted as traveling to the summit in June 2000 with the sinister goal of dragging the DPRK into the "free world." (The scare quotes are the Text's.) He even rehearses the talks beforehand with Kim Jong Il impersonators or *kagemusha*, the better to sharpen his skills of persuasion.[9] (The Japanese word underscores the un-Korean deviousness of the exercise.) Days before the trip, his men trumpet their anti-communism in the "national assembly." They will dangle aid in front of the North Koreans in the hope that the country's economic difficulties will make them yield to the South's proposals.

The plan backfires. Arriving at the airport in Pyongyang, Kim Dae Jung is stunned to find the smiling General waiting to greet him. Unmanned by this unprecedented departure from North Korean protocol, the doddering "president" cuts an even more pathetic figure than usual. In the following excerpt, which retains the bold font use of the original text, a journalist from Seoul remembers with embarrassment how Kim Dae Jung reviewed the DPRK's honor guard:

> The forest of serried bayonets gleaming in the sunshine! The "president" hobbling along on his ailing legs!!... We were used to seeing him walking with effort.... But at that moment we felt sorry for him...sad ... uneasy. Because it looked as if the old "president" was flustered. But I felt something shooting up inside me when I saw National Defense Council Chairman Kim Jong Il walking at a deeply considerate pace behind him, saw his courteous, polite form....[10]

The two men get into a limousine that takes them into Pyongyang down a road lined with crowds shouting the Dear Leader's (and only his) name. Later, at a banquet, the "president"'s wife sits at a remove from the two men; the novel contrives to imply that all is not well in the south Koreans' marriage. The Dear Leader asks her to come and join them. "We can't be having divided families even in the banquet hall," he jokes, as the room erupts in laughter.[11] On another occasion he peremptorily calls out "Come here, ministers!" to the top-ranking members of the south Korean delegation. The Text claims that schoolteachers in Seoul now use the phrase when summoning their little charges: "The kids get a kick out of it."[12]

The "president" is described as having been thwarted by the genius and charisma of the Dear Leader, who, instead of yielding to Seoul in return for handouts, demanded economic *cooperation*—and got it. He demanded a joint declaration of the need for autonomy and unification—and got that too.[13] Of course, to say that the south Korean officials had been persuaded by rational argument would be to imply that they a) were reasonable people, b) had the autonomy to sign inter-Korean agreements as they saw fit, and c) might henceforth agree with the DPRK on some issues. These are all potentially subversive notions. One is therefore to believe that the visitors were somehow dazzled and befuddled into signing on the dotted line, then "came to" during the return to Seoul, where popular "Kim Jong Il mania" kept them from reneging on the agreement.†

In short, the Dear Leader won this zero-sum game and the "president" lost. The south Korean journalist sums up:

> "We conducted all manner of preparation and research to pull the North into the 'free world.' But in the event, not only we but the whole of 'Han'guk' were unexpectedly swept up in Kim Jong Il mania. There's no knowing what power it was that turned everything on its head in a moment…. [W]e cannot but admit that our 'peace strategy' has suffered a total defeat at the hands of the North's autonomy strategy."[14]

This is not pure fantasy. Judging from the South Koreans photographed at the summit, whose star-struck faces would not look out of place on a Pyongyang subway mural, the Leader did indeed succeed in charming his guests. He won over millions of television-watchers in the ROK too. (Schoolgirls there began describing him as "cute.")[15] But there was nothing like the mass frenzy described in the novel,

† Much the same motivation was behind propaganda about the US-DPRK talks of the mid-1990s; it was gloatingly claimed that American negotiators had signed an agreement disastrously unfavorable to their side. See for example, *Ryŏksa ŭi taeha*, 496.

which talks of young Seoulites adopting the General's spartan work uniform, plum-tinted glasses selling like hotcakes, and crowds piling raucously into restaurants to eat Pyongyang-style noodles.[16] Young lovers take advantage of the auspicious event to get married, posing for wedding photographs before backdrops of People's Army soldiers.[17] One man drives around with the DPRK's flag fluttering from his hood.[18] (When it suits the North to exaggerate the freedom of expression enjoyed in the South, it does so; in the real ROK, flying the red star of the rival state remains a punishable offense.) No one spares a thought for the feeble "president." Truly, the summit was "a meeting between the Dear Leader and the 40 million-strong masses (minjung) of the south."[19]

As with the American enemy, the South Korean government's gestures of good will are attributed to fear of the DPRK's superior might and resolve. Kim Dae Jung's repatriation of North Korean spies after the 2000 summit is a case in point: "The [southern] authorities bowed to pressure from the Republic's government."[20] The following excerpt from the oft-reprinted novel *World of Stars* (Pyŏl ŭi segye, 2002) recounts the Dear Leader's response to the news.

Propaganda now concedes South Korea's superior material wealth while still claiming that people there yearn to live under Pyongyang's rule. Above, a street in Seoul erupts in joy at televised footage of Kim Jong Il.

Comrade Kim Jong Il quickly skimmed the report. For a moment a smile crossed his face. "They had no choice. Hm. Well, take a look. They're finally bowing down." All eyes turned to the document. Soon their faces, too—faces that had been taut with excitement and tension—were wreathed in smiles…. "Comrade Supreme Commander, the bastards, their backs against the wall, made this decision out of fear, didn't they?" "Yes, it's true," someone cried. "It looks like they were frightened of us, all right." Comrade Kim Jong Il just kept on smiling.[21]

At another point in the novel, the South (now under Kim Dae Jung's rule) requests that the North do a little repatriating of its own. One of the Dear Leader's officials is stunned by this presumption:

> "General," he said falteringly. "They're saying they're going to apply their principle of 'reciprocity' even to the issue of the long-term prisoners they couldn't convert, so it looks like once again we're going to have to..." [Kim Jong Il:] "Make them eat another hard blow? Of course we have to do that."[22]

The Text continues to remind the public of how much North Korea's heroic returnees suffered in captivity.[23] Always the unchanging nature of the Yankee colony is stressed: "The 'government' can change ten, twenty times, and America will still be calling the shots," according to *The Letter* (2005).[24]

And yet this line never prevented the regime from claiming, especially in material aimed at South Korean readers, that an accession to power by the right-wing Grand National Party would plunge the peninsula into another ruinous war. These "Yankee lackeys" are described in the Text as a lunatic fringe able to wield political influence only due to their close ties to Washington. The election of a conservative to the South Korean presidency in 2007 thus forced the propaganda apparatus to claim that "the traitor Lee Myung Bak" had deceived voters about his true intentions. The following is from the KCNA's English-language service:

Propaganda celebrated the defeat of the South Korean right in regional elections on April 29, 2009, but President Lee Myung Bak, shown here in the noose, had already begun rising in opinion polls—much to the DPRK's consternation.

As far as Lee Myung Bak is concerned, he is a conservative political charlatan who took the office of mayor of Seoul from the ticket of the GNP after doing business since the period of the "Yusin" fascist dictatorial regime *[of Park Chung Hee—BRM]*. No wonder he revealed his true colors as a sycophant towards the US and anti-north confrontation advocator as soon as he came to power.[25]

Though massive street protests in Seoul against American beef imports in 2008 seemed to confirm this propaganda line for a while, they were quick to fade away, and Lee's approval ratings have since climbed steadily. A popular conservative president in the South, and the information cordon too full of holes to keep the North Korean masses ignorant of him: the propaganda apparatus seems at a loss to deal with this unprecedented state of affairs. In apparent desperation it has reverted to preposterous, pre-2000 style claims of widespread South Korean poverty.[26] Thus does the regime run the risk of forfeiting the credibility it managed to maintain for so long, but what choice does it have? Even if Lee's popularity declines again, it is but a matter of time before most North Koreans realize that the southern brethren are proud of their state, indifferent to the Dear Leader's very existence, and content to postpone reunification indefinitely. Such revelations may not bring down the regime at once, but they will certainly bring down the Text.

CONCLUSION

"Kim Jong Il doesn't believe that stuff himself," an American diplomat cheerfully told me in 2005 after I had finished a lecture on North Korean ideology. "He told Madeleine Albright it's all fake." Many in Washington evidently think the same way. Indeed, America has so far negotiated with Pyongyang under the apparent conviction that the regime believes the *opposite* of what it tells its subjects. The louder the Text calls for a "blood reckoning" with the Yankee enemy, the more firmly Washington believes that the DPRK wants better relations. At a government-sponsored conference in Washington in 2008 I heard more than one Pyongyang watcher argue that Kim Jong Il wants America *as an ally.*

The obvious retort to this wishful thinking is to ask how the DPRK could possibly justify its existence after giving up the confrontational anti-Americanism that constitutes its last remaining source of legitimacy. We are dealing here with a failure not just of information analysis but of common sense—a failure to understand that North Korea is one of two states laying claim to the same nation. It must either go on convincing its citizens that it is the better Korea or acknowledge Seoul's right to rule the whole peninsula. This is why it is so futile for the West to promise Pyongyang aid and assistance in return for disarmament. As if the poorer Korea could trade a heroic nationalist mission for mere economic growth without its subjects opting for immediate absorption by the rival state! But let us assume, for the sake of argument, that the regime in Pyongyang is as unaware of this problem as so many outside observers seem to be. The question still arises why it would enshrine the military-first principle in the DPRK constitution, groom the putative successor as yet another invincible General, and continue demonizing America as the eternal race enemy, if it had not already rejected the possibility of a fundamental change in policy.

Some might insist on the unlikelihood of such a manifestly intelligent leader, such an urbane and well-informed ruling elite, such a literate and resourceful populace genuinely believing things that everyone else in the world finds so irrational. But if outside observers knew

North Korean ideology better, they would understand (as I trust the reader of the preceding chapters has understood) that it is not as irrational as all that. Praising a leader as the perfect embodiment of ethnic virtues is less extravagant than praising him, as Stalin was praised, as the highest authority in every science. One could also argue that there is at least more historical justification for the DPRK's anti-Americanism than many other states have had for their own hatemongering campaigns. Paranoid nationalism may well be an intellectual void, and appeal to the lowest instincts—there is nothing in North Korean ideology that a child of twelve cannot grasp at once—but for that very reason it has proven itself capable of uniting citizens of all classes, and inspiring them through bad times as well as good ones.

As I explained in the historical part of this book, the regime was very quick to adjust its claims downward when it had to, i.e. in response to post-Soviet economic realities and the influx of heterodox information. But to concede the regime's genius for propaganda—a genius which only now seems to be deserting it—is not to imply that it does not believe the official myths itself. Could it be any clearer that in its relations with the outside world, the leadership practices what it preaches in the Text, and not what it tells impressionable foreign visitors behind closed doors? Barely-veiled hostility to allies and aid providers, terrorist adventurism and drug-running, blithe indifference to trade and debt obligations, abortions forced on returnees from China—whence does this unique pattern of behavior derive, if not from the belief that the world's "cleanest, most civilized people" can and indeed *must* play by its own rules? What other kind of regime would be able to boast to its own people that it had signed a nuclear treaty in bad faith?

* * *

I have dwelt in this book on the continuity between the imperial Japanese worldview instilled into colonial-era Koreans and the official North Korean worldview that immediately succeeded it. This racialism is utterly irreconcilable with Marx and Lenin; not for nothing was the DPRK almost as isolated from the rest of the East Bloc as it still is from the West. But while drawing a clear line between North Korean ideology and communism, we should not overlook that which distinguishes the former from Japanese and (even more so) German fascism. The Text has never proposed the invasion of so much as an inch of non-Korean territory, let alone the permanent subjugation of foreign peoples. This is not to say that it does not propose military action against the US either as a pre-emptive strike or as revenge for past crimes. (I have already mentioned the wish-fulfilling posters of the US Capitol being blown to pieces.) But this is not the same as wanting to re-shape the world. Where the Nazis considered the Aryans physically and intellectually superior to all other races, and the Japanese regarded their moral superiority as having protected them throughout history, the Koreans believe that their childlike purity renders them so vulnerable to the outside world that they need a Parent Leader to survive. Such a worldview naturally precludes dreams of a colonizing or imperialist nature.

This does not make North Korea any less of a threat to South Korea—or vice versa. At present the DPRK's main security problem is not America, but the prosperity of the other Korean state, whose citizens are content to prolong the division of the peninsula indefinitely. This is another reason why Pyongyang cannot normalize relations with Washington: the Text would never survive the North Korean masses' inevitable realization that it was their own blood brothers and not the Yankees who had been blocking reunification all along. From the North's perspective, America's friendship would be—to paraphrase something Burke once said of revolutionary France—more dangerous than its enmity.

Pyongyang therefore negotiates with Washington not to defuse tension but to manage it, to keep it from tipping into all-out war or an equally perilous all-out peace. Ignorant of this, because ignorant of the North's ideology, Americans tend to blame problems in US-DPRK relations on whoever happens to be in the Oval Office, thinking him either too soft or too hard on Pyongyang. The right talks in moralistic terms of Kim Jong Il's evil and perfidy in refusing to disarm, with no apparent understanding that he *cannot* disarm and hope to stay in power. The left, meanwhile, continues to call for bold American trust-building measures.[1] In doing so, it overlooks the failure of the ROK's Sunshine Policy (a decade of generous and unconditional aid) to generate even a modicum of good will from the North. To expect Washington to succeed with Pyongyang where the South Korean left failed is to take American exceptionalism to a new extreme. The unpleasant truth is that one can neither bully nor cajole a regime—least of all one with nuclear weapons—into committing political suicide.

Much hope in the West centers on the infiltration of heterodox culture into the DPRK, but here too it would be folly to extrapolate from Cold War history. Blue jeans will not bring down *this* dictatorship. Race-based nationalism does not need to fear cultural subversion as much as Marxism-Leninism did. Hollywood films were all the rage in imperial Japan, and Luftwaffe aces famously flew into battle with Mickey Mouse painted on their fuselages. More to the point, perhaps, South Koreans were as ready in 2008 to believe that America was saving its deadliest beef for their consumption as they were in 2002 to believe that US soldiers had run over two schoolgirls for the fun of it. Anti-Japanese sentiment, for its part, has actually *increased* in the ROK since a ban on Japanese cultural imports was lifted several years ago. There is little reason, therefore, to believe that smuggled CDs and DVDs will undermine the average North Korean's hostility to the outside world.

The DPRK is more likely to suffer a mass legitimation crisis if it is seen as failing on its own ideological terms. Such a perception could result from a humiliating retreat in regard to nuclear weapons, but the North Korean leadership is less likely than our own to make that kind of error. The chronic nature of the economic malaise poses a greater problem. It is all well and good for the military-first regime to shrug off responsibility for such matters, but if the acquisition of a nuclear deterrent constituted such a glorious victory over the US, where, the malnourished citizen may well ask, are the material fruits of that victory?

But most dangerous to the regime, as I have already said, is the inevitable spread of public awareness that for all their anti-Americanism, the South Koreans are happy with their own republic and do not want to live under Pyongyang's rule. There is just no way for the Text to make sense of this highly subversive truth. We should not, however, sit back and gloat over the regime's troubles, because it is bound to counter any sign of internal unrest by ratcheting up tension with America or South Korea. The result could well be a serious conflict or even another attempt at "liberating" the South. While I take the experts' word for it that the DPRK would be unable to beat either of its arch-rivals, I do not share their confidence that it would never be foolish enough to try. Although the anti-American and pro-North sentiments expressed in South Korean opinion polls are belied by the continued lack of support for a US troop pull-out, the DPRK has at least as much reason to expect a liberator's welcome as America had in 2003 when it invaded Iraq.[2] In any case, the prevalence of motherly authority figures, the glorification of "pure" racial instincts, the denigration of reason and restraint—all these things encourage rashness among the DPRK's decision-makers just as they encourage spontaneous violence among average North Koreans. We must be careful what we wish for.

NOTES

Preface

1. Ramstad, "Gulags, Nukes and a Water Slide," *Wall Street Journal*, May 22, 2009.
2. Sternhell, "Fascist Ideology," 318.
3. Schurmann, *Ideology and Organization in Communist China*, 507.
4. Myers, "Ideology as Smokescreen: North Korea's Juche Thought," 161-182.
5. As Alfred Pfabigan noted in regard to his stay in Pyongyang in 1982, "all information that my minders give me, all memorial sites that I visit, all the teachings that are conveyed to me, are contained in the president's biography." *Schlaflos in Pjöngjang*, 58.
6. Propaganda published before the cultural revolution of the mid-1960s cannot be accessed even by the general public.
7. I have also been fortunate enough to visit North Korea on more than one occasion, the last time having been a day trip to Kaesong in 2008.
8. Myers, *Han Sŏrya and North Korean Literature*, 1994.

Chapter One
The Colonial Era, 1910-1945

1. See Mansourov, "Lessons of History and Contemporary Challenges in Korean-Chinese Relations," *Harvard Asia Quarterly*, 1/2006.
2. Eckert, *The Koch'ang Kims*, 226. See also Shin, *Ethnic Nationalism in Korea*, 5-6.
3. On Japanese claims to an inherent moral superiority over other races, see Dower, *War Without Mercy*, 205.
4. It was a desire to reduce the Korean language to the status of a dialect, and not to stamp it out entirely, which induced the colonial authorities to crack down on its use in schools. Song Min-ho, *Iljemal amhŭkki munhak yŏn'gu*, 47, 49.
5. Yi Yŏng-hun, "Wae tashi haebang chŏnhusa inga," 33. The original legend did not specify the mountain on which Tan'gun was born.
6. Ibid.
7. Song, *Iljemal amhŭkki munhak yŏn'gu*, 288.
8. Cho, "'Minjok ŭi him ŭl yongmanghan 'ch'inil naesyŏnŏlisŭt'ŭ' Yi Kwang-su," 548-552.

9. Song, 133.

10. *Singminji Chosŏn kwa chŏnjaeng misul,* 145, 114.

11. Kim Ch'ŏl, "Mollakhanŭn sinsaeng – 'Manju ŭi kkum kwa <nonggun> ŭi odok," *Haebang chŏnhusa,* 479-523.

12. Song, 87, 90-91, 124. See also Cho, 548.

13. "Kara! Ch' ŏngnyŏn hakdoyŏ," in *Maeil sinbo,* November 20, 1943.

14. Cho, 524-555.

15. This is not to assume, as so much South Korean historiography does, that the masses were nationalists.

16. Ellul, *Propaganda,* 108-109.

17. Song, 127-128.

18. Ibid., 46.

19. Chŏn Kwang-yong, in his famous short story, "Kapitan Ri" (1962), *Land of Exile, Contemporary Korean Fiction,* 63.

20. Song, 127.

21. Ch'oi, "Chŏllyŏk chŭnggang ch'onghu suho ŭi chillo," *Maeil sinbo,* March 7, 1945.

22. Lankov, *From Stalin to Kim Il Sung,* 11.

The Soviet Occupation, 1945-1948

1. Ch'oi Kyŏng-hŏi, "Ch'inil munhak ŭi tto tarŭn ch' ŭngwi," 389-391.

2. Lankov, *From Stalin to Kim Il Sung,* 9.

3. Ibid., 10.

4. Han Pyŏng-gu, "Pukhan ŭi sinmun," 92-93.

5. Kang, "Pukhan ŭi pangsong," 155.

6. See Lankov, *From Stalin to Kim,* 49-76, for an excellent concise biography of Kim.

7. Lankov, *From Stalin to Kim,* 40. Nor should one assume (as the Soviet administration appear to have done) that the Soviet-Koreans arriving in Pyongyang were any better trained. Hwang Chang-yŏp writes that Marxism was taught in North Korea's early years by Soviet-Koreans who showed no understanding of it themselves. Hwang, *Hwoigorok,* 122.

8. *Chosŏn chŏnsa,* 23: 300.

9. Sin Chu-hyŏn, "Kim Il-sŏng, ch'inil int'elli to kanbu ro tŭngyong hetta," dailynk.com, September 16, 2005.

10. Kenez, *The Birth of the Propaganda State,* 5, 8-9.

11. Ch'oi had once danced for Hitler. For more information on the former collaborators in the North Korean cultural apparatus, see Myers, *Han Sŏrya*, 38-39.

12. Lankov, *From Stalin to Kim Il Sung*, 39-40.

13. "Munhwa wa yesul ŭn inmin ŭl wihan kŏs ŭro toeŏya handa," 96-104.

14. Hyŏn, *Chŏkch'i yungnyŏn Pukhan ŭi mundan*, 50-51.

15. Ibid., 25.

16. For more on this anthology see Myers, *Han Sŏrya*, 46-47.

17. The original legend had not identified the mountain on which Tan'gun had been born.

18. See, for example, the picture of a Korean girl tied to a rotary grain mill in Bratzke, *Kita Chosen 'rakuen' no zangai*, 109.

19. Ch'oi, "Kangje tongwŏn chŏnbŏm omyŏng pŏsŏtta," November 13, 2006.

20. See for example Han Sŏr-ya's *Nammae* (1949), or Yi Ch'un-jin, *Anna* (1948); both are short stories.

21. For relevant excerpts see Myers, "Mother Russia: Soviet Characters in North Korean Fiction," 82-93.

22. Han Sŏr-ya, *Nammae*, 174.

23. *Postwar*, 61.

24. Gabroussenko, *Soldiers on the Cultural Front* (manuscript), page 24 of Chapter 2.

25. Han, *Hyŏllo*, 24.

26. Gabroussenko, *Soldiers*, page 35 of Chapter 2.

27. Han, *Ryŏksa*, 114.

28. Gabroussenko, 117.

29. Kimura Mitsuhiko, "P'asijŭm esŏ kongsanjuŭi ro," 737-764.

30. Cf. Dower, 191.

31. Admiringly quoted by Han Sŏr-ya in, "Kim Il-sŏng changgun kwa minjok munhwa ŭi palchŏn," 28.

32. Hyŏn, 42.

War and Reconstruction, 1948-1966

1. Weathersby, "Korea, 1949-50: To Attack, or Not to Attack?" 1-9.

2. Sin, "Sinin'gan," 733-734; Gabroussenko, *Soldiers*, 25-27.

3. See Shen, "Sino-North Korean Conflict and its Resolution," 9-38.

4. The speech in question is "Chŏnch'e chakka yesulgadŭl ege," in *Kim Il-sŏng sŏnjip*, 3:242-244.

5. Kim Sa-ryang, "Uri nŭn irŏk'e igyŏtta," in *Kim Sa-ryang sŏnjip* (Pyongyang, 1955), 341-369. The latter story is Yi T'ae-jun's "Miguk taesagwan." Gabroussenko, *Soldiers* (manuscript), page 32 of Chapter 4. The story would never have been published had it not pleased the party, and it was rumored to have been enjoyed by Kim Il Sung himself. But the unchivalrous conduct of the story's Korean characters was held against the author during his purge in 1956. Gabroussenko, *Soldiers* (MS), chapter 4.

6. Han Sŏr-ya, "Pabo k'ongk'ŭl," 293.

7. For a complete translation see my *Han Sŏrya and North Korean Literature*, 157-188.

8. Shen, 19-20.

9. Myers, "The Watershed that Wasn't," 101-103.

10. Lankov, *Crisis in North Korea*, 29.

11. Gabroussenko, 129; Szalontai, *Kim Il Sung*, 89.

12. Schäfer, "Weathering the Sino-Soviet Conflict," 40.

13. Ibid., 39.

14. Ibid., 40; Szalontai, "You Have No Political Line of Your Own," 98.

15. Szalontai, *Kim Il Sung*, 98-100.

16. Schäfer, "Weathering the Sino-Soviet Conflict," 33.

17. Szalontai, *Kim Il Sung*, 251.

18. Schäfer, "Weathering the Sino-Soviet Conflict," 30.

19. Szalontai, "You Have No Political Line of Your Own," 131.

20. Szalontai, *Kim*, 201, 55. The American Black Panther Eldridge Cleaver visited Pyongyang in 1970 and later complained about the "unsubtle racism" of his hosts. *Soul on Fire*, 122;

21. "Document No. 3: Report, GDR Embassy in the DPRK, 2 April 1965," 43.

From the Cultural Revolution to Kim Il Sung's Death , 1966-1994

1. See Schäfer, "North Korean 'Adventurism' and China's Long Shadow, 1966-1972," in particular the first chapter, 3-16.

2. Hwang Chang-yŏp describes the events of the latter half of the 1960s as a "miniature version" of China's Cultural Revolution. Hwang, *Hoigorok*, 187.

3. Ironically enough, the movie was an enormous hit in China too; the novelist Tie Ning describes a theater full of weeping Beijing residents in her well-known short story "How Long is Forever?" (Yingyuan you duo yuan, 1999).

4. Kim is said to have led troops on a march across north-east China in the winter of 1938/39.

5. Hwang Chang-yŏp asserts that Kim relied heavily on a team of speechwriters and ghostwriters, asking them to "read" the unexpressed ideas in his head. Hwang, *Hoigorok*, 136.

6. For a longer discussion of the speech, see Myers, "The Watershed that Wasn't," *Acta Koreana*, January 2006, 89-115. See also Zagoria, 11-12.

7. Hwang Chang-yŏp, *Huigorok*, 195-196.

8. Kim Il Sung, "Uri tang ŭi chuch'e sasang," 27:394-395.

9. Cumings, *Origins of the Korean War*, 2:313.

10. See for example Harrison, *Korean Endgame*, 21-22.

11. See for example "Widaehan ŏmŏni tang," *Rodong sinmun*, October 3 2003, and "*Rodong sinmun* on Role Played by WPK as Mother Party," KCNA, December 14, 2007.

12. Sŏ Sŏng-nyong, "Pom hanŭl," in *Ch'ŏngnyŏn munhak*, October 1990, 11.

13. Maggie Jones, "Shutting Themselves In," *The New York Times*, January 15, 2006.

14. Having worked in the late 1990s in China for a German car-maker, I well remember hearing colleagues marvel at the North Koreans' orders of large numbers of luxury sedans.

15. Haggard and Noland, 27.

16. "By 1993 imports from Russia were only 10 percent of their average 1987-90 level." Noland, *Avoiding the Apocalypse*, 98.

17. Ibid., 58. The "campaign for emulating hidden heroes" had been formally launched back in 1979. *A Handbook on North Korea*, 89.

The Arduous March, 1994-1998

1. *Ch'inaehanŭn chidoja Kim Jŏng-il tongji ŭi t'ansaeng 50 tol* (70 minutes), Pyongyang, 1972.

2. See the novel *Yŏngsaeng* (1997) for the standard account of the events of 1993/94.

3. See for example, "K'ŭnak'ŭn ŭnjŏng ŭl norae hanŭn p'ungnyŏn taeji," *Rodong sinmun*, September 2, 1994.

4. *Pukhan chumin ŭi ilsang saenghwal kwa taejung munha*, 29.

5. Hwang's autobiography confirms widespread refugee reports of human flesh being passed off as animal meat in city markets. *Hoigorok*, 349.

6. Haggard and Noland, for example, estimate that the famine killed between 600,000 and one million people. *Famine in North Korea*, 1.

7. Shin, *Ethnic Nationalism in Korea*, 93.

8. See Yi U-yŏng, *Pukhan ŭi chabonjuŭi insik pyŏnhwa*, Seoul, 2000, 15.

9. War is a common "flight-from-grief device" in tribes going through extreme hardship. Turney-High, *Primitive War*, 142.

The Sunshine Years, 1998-2008

1. "Uri ŭi kangnyŏkhan chŏnjaeng ŏkcheryŏk ŭn Chosŭn pando p'yŏnghwa ŭi tambo ida," KCNA, May 28, 2003.

2. *Ch'ŏllima*, August 2003, 49-59; *Adong munhak*, August 2003, 48-56; *Chosŏn munhak*, August 2003, 44-61.

3. "Haksŭp chegang: isaekchŏgin saenghwal p'ungjo rŭl yup'o sik'inŭn chŏkdŭl ŭi ch'aekdong ŭl ch'ŏlchŏhi chitpusilte taehayŏ," Pyongyang, 2005, 1. There is no reason to doubt the authenticity of the document, not least because it would be much less dull and repetitive if someone had forged it!

4. Ibid., 3-4.

5. Ibid., 4.

6. "Underground Christians Keep Faith in a Hostile North Korea," Doug Struck, *Washington Post*, April 12, 2001.

7. Good Friends, 72.

8. "2005-nyŏn Pukhan." *Chosŏn ilbo*, December 12, 2004.

PART II

Chapter Two

1. "Two Koreas' Top Brass Resort to Racist Mudslinging," *Chosun Ilbo* (English Language Edition), May 17, 2006.

2. This practice is still going strong. See for example the reference to North Korea as a "secretive Stalinist state" in Harden, "All Nuclear Efforts Disclosed, North Korea Says," *Washington Post*, January 5, 2008.

3. Ch'oi, "'Ta'minjok, tainjong sahoe,'" *Rodong sinmun*, April 27, 2006.

4. Sternhell, "Fascist Ideology," 324.

5. Between January 1996 and December 2006 there were 575 KCNA articles referring to the motherland, and 1,930 referring to the fatherland. And yet one finds references to a motherland in other English-language sources, such as Choe In Su's official biography of Kim Jong Il (see page 5 and elsewhere).

6. See for example, Sŏ Man-sul, "Ŏmŏni choguk e tŭrinŭn kŭl," *Rodong sinmun*, September 17, 2003.

7. Pang Chae-sun, "Choguk ŭi p'um," 70.

8. This summary derives primarily from the entry on Korean history in the official encyclopedia, *Chosŏn taebaekkwa sajŏn*, 18:118-193.

9. *The Denial of Death*, 133.

10. There is a photograph in *Chosŏn taebaekkwa sajŏn*, *18:128*.

11. *Ethnonationalism*, 140.

12. North Korea's first constitution (1948) still designated Seoul as the republic's capital.

13. "P'yŏngyang ŭi nunbora," 145.

14. "Chin'gyŏk ŭi narut'ŏ" (1971), in *Pukhan misul 50-nyŏn*, 144.

15. See the painting "Yugyŏk kŭn'gŏji naekka'esŏ" (1970) in *Pukhan misul 50-nyŏn*, 84. Kim Jong Il notoriously told Kim Dae Jung during the 2000 summit that women should stay home and do laundry. Ch'oi Chin-hŭi, "Puk ŭi yŏsŏng ch'abyŏl ŭn chongnyu to mant'a," Nkchosun.com. August 5, 2005.

16. The motif of a South Korean man rescuing a countrywoman from a gang of menacing foreigners has been a staple of TV dramas for decades, as in the KBS drama *Sarang handa, mian hada* (Sorry, I love you, 2004).

17. Kim Il Sung quoted in *Widaehan suryŏng Kim Il-sŏng tongji ŭi pulmyŏl ŭi hyŏngmyŏng ŏpchŏk*, 13. Kim Jong Il quoted in "Usuhan minjok yusan ŭi kalp'i sok esŏ," *Ch'ŏllima*, November 2006, 87.

18. *Chosŏn taebaekkwa sajŏn*, 18:125. See for example the entry for Confucianism (yugyo) in the same source, 26:353. Whereas serious historians in South Korea do not attribute an obsession

with female modesty and chastity to all of Yi Dynasty society, but only to the Confucian *yangban* class, the North Koreans regard it as an instinct inherent to the entire race.

19. See for example Na P'ung-man's short story, "Kong e kittŭn iyagi," (1975), in the anthology *Kŭm medal ŭi muge*, Pyongyang, 2006, page 30. In the visual arts the North Koreans are shown towering over insect-like Yankees, but this is of course purely symbolic.

20. Kim is quoted in *Chosŏn taebaekkwa sajŏn*, 18:118; "*Rodong sinmun* on Korean People's Inexhaustible Mental Power," KCNA, January 29, 2008. The article makes clear that the Korean people's perseverance and fighting spirit are meant, not any special intelligence.

21. *T'aeyang sungbae ŭi yŏngwŏnhan hwap'ok*, 42-44; Bratzke, *Kita Chōsen 'rakuen' no zangai*, 109.

22. Ryang, "The Great Mother Party" (Widaehan ŏmŏni tang), *Rodong sinmun*, October 3, 2003.

23. The poet is Kim Ch'ŏl. See "Kŭ p'um ŭl ttŏna mot sara sŏjŏngsi ŏmŏni rŭl ŭlp'ŭmyŏ," KCNA, October 9 2003; "ŏmŏni," *Ch'ŏllima*, October 2005, 12-13.

24. Fromm, *Heart of Man*, 107.

25. Weber, "Revolution? Counterrevolution? What Revolution?" 438.

26. Clark, *The Soviet Novel*, 15ff.

27. This "master plot" dates back to the very beginnings of so-called "proletarian" fiction in the 1920s.

28. "Kukchejŏk myŏnmo katchwŏganŭn P'yŏngyang yŏnghwa ch'ukchŏn," Nkchosun.com, September 20, 2004.

29. The South's Caucasian-style ideal, in contrast, is attainable only through plastic surgery.

30. "Nuga pwado choŭn tchalpŭn mŏri hyŏngt'ae," *Ch'ŏllima*, Jan 2005, 97.

31. *Kongsanjuŭi todŏk*, 1995, 1:4-5.

32. July 22, 2009. The nightly news usually closes with one or two maxims attributed to Kim Jong Il.

33. See, for example, the short story "Transition," which is discussed in the chapter on Kim Jong Il.

34. This is a lyric from the song, "Let Us Venerate the Supreme Commander With Our Weapons" (*"Mujang ŭro patt ŭlja, uri ŭi ch'oigo saryŏnggwan."*)

35. Han Sŏr-ya, *Ryŏksa*, 57.

36. "Ttangk' ŭ 214 ho," 563.

37. "Sajin sogae," *Ch'ŏllima*, January 2005, 5-8.

38. "Changbyŏngdŭl ŭi hwanhosŏng," *Ch'ŏllima*, August 2006, 24.

39. "Kunmin ilch'i ro sŭngni rŭl haja," *Rodong sinmun*, May 26, 1998.

40. Pauer, *Japan's War Economy*, 2-3.

41. The most famous North Korean film version is *Love, Love, My Love* (Sarang, sarang, nae sarang, 1984).

42. See the film *My Happiness* (Na ŭi haengbok, 1988), which deals with a female military doctor.

43. Kim Il Sung, "Chosŏn rodongdang che 4-ch'a taehoe esŏ," 15:189.

44. See for example Yi Ki-yŏng's novel *Ttang*, 442-444, or Han Sŏr-ya's *Charanŭn maŭl*, 265.

45. Specific reference is made here to Ri Ryul-sŏn's land-reclamation-themed painting *Kansŏkchi kaegan* (1961), Ch'oi Kye-gŭn's painting *Yonghaegong* (1968), in *Pukhan misul 50-nyŏn*, pages 132 and 41 respectively, and to the film *Kalmaegi ho ch'ŏngnyŏndŭl* (1961).

46. *Toraji kkot'*, 1988, *Tosi ch'ŏnyŏ sijip wayo!* 1993.

47. The classic examples are Mikhail Sholokhov's *Virgin Soil Under the Plough* (Podnyataya tselina, 1932), and Ding Ling's *The Sun Shines Over the Sanggan River* (Taiyang zhao zai Sangganhe shang, 1948).

48. The scene comes in the latter half of *My Happiness* (Na ŭi haengbok, 1988).

49. *Ch'ukbok hamnida*, 2001.

50. Han Yun, *Ssiat*, 34.

51. The novel became a bestseller in South Korea. Hong Sŏk-chung, *Hwang Jin'i*, Seoul, 2003.

52. See *The Bellflower* (Toraji kkot', 1988).

53. Han Sŏr-ya, "Hugi," in *Chŏngch'un'gi*, 398.

54. See also Paek Nam-nyong, *Pŏt*, 1988.

55. "Sahoejuŭi hyŏnsil ŭl panyŏnghan hyŏngmyŏngjŏk yŏnghwa rŭl tŏ manhi ch'angjak haja," 89.

56. Hwang, "Tasi toraon taramjui," *Adong munhak*, December 2005, 42-45.

57. Typical is *My Happiness* (Naŭi haengbok, 1988).

Chapter Three

1. See for example Thomas Hosuck Kang's *Why the North Koreans Behave as They Do* (1994), and Selig Harrison's *Korean Endgame*, 21-24. Cumings advances much the same message in *Korea's Place in the Sun*, 415-418. Typical journalistic references to North Korea's Confucian tendencies: McCormack, "Book Talk," ABC Radio National, March 1, 2003.

2. Mark Clifford, "A Nation of Famine and Adulation: Letter from Pyongyang," *Business Week*, December 18, 2000; Erik Cornell, "An Oddly Troublesome Couple," *The Daily Times* (Australia), January 29, 2003.

3. Harrison, *Korean Endgame*, 21.

4. My main source for this summary is the entry on Kim Il Sung in *Chosŏn taebaekkwa sajŏn*, 1:3-17. For part of the paragraph on his childhood, I drew from Han Sŏrya's *Man'gyŏngdae* (1955) 362-491; for Kim's early rising, see *Yŏngsaeng*, 1997, 7. For the ash tree reference, see Choe, *Kim Jong Il*, 9.

5. In 2007 the seventieth (!) volume of the *Among the Masses* (Inmindŭl sok esŏ, 1962–) series of "on-the-spot guidance" story anthologies was published.

6. "Myŏng'ŏn haesŏl," *Ch'ŏngnyŏn munhak*, March 2004, 18.

7. *Chosŏn taebaekkwa sajŏn*, 18:154.

8. Myers, *Han Sŏrya*, 136-137.

9. *Chosŏn taebaekkwa sajŏn*, 18:193.

10. Han Sŏr-ya, *Hyŏllo*, 24.

11. *Chosŏn taebaekkwa sajŏn*, 18:194.

12. Choe, *Kim Jong Il*, 21.

13. *Kim Jong Suk, Mother of Korea*, 92.

14. See a famous "photograph" of Kim and his wife during the guerilla years, ibid., 18:195.

15. Han Sŏrya, *Ryŏksa*, 114.

16. See Chŏng Kwan-ch'ŏl's canonical painting, "Poch'ŏnbo ŭi hwappul," on the frontispiece of Yi, *Pukhan misurŭi 50 nyŏn*.

17. *4 ch'ŏnman ŭi t'aeyang*, 2:23.

18. Kim Kyu-hak, Kim Ki-chŏl, "10 wŏl ŭi hwanho," *Pukhan misul ŭi 50-nyŏn*, 116.

19. See, for example, Han Sŏrya's short story "Kaesŏn" (1948).

20. See for example the cartoon "Wihŏmhan pul changnan," on page 59 of *Ch' ŏllima*, June 1998, or the illustrations of the American missionary in the short story *Jackals* (Sŭngnyangi), in *Adong Munhak*, August 2003, 48.

21. In *My Happiness* (Na ŭi haengbok, 1988), a KPA soldier shouts these words before blowing up herself and a South Korean gunship. "Suryŏngnim, ap' e nŭn ch'oichŏnsŏn imnida" in *Chosŏn yesul*, July 1982, 18.

22. "Suryŏngnim, ap' e nŭn ch'oichŏnsŏn imnida" in *Chosŏn yesul*, July 1982, 18.

23. "Lots of Literary Works Praising Kim Jong Il Created," KCNA, August 23, 2007.

24. See *Pukhan misul ŭi 50 nyŏn*, 7 and 124.

25. Kang Ch'ŏr-wŏn, "3-dae rŭl iŏ angyŏ chusin sarang kwa ŭnjŏng," 181.

26. See the painting, "Kwan'gae kongsajang ŭl hyŏnji jido hayŏ chusinŭn Kim Il-sŏng tongji," in *Chosŏn yesul*, March 1982, front matter.

27. Sŏ Kwang-sŏn, "Yŏnp'ung chunghakkyo e saegyŏjin sarang ŭi chŏnsŏl," 159.

28. *Chosŏn taebaekkwa sajŏn*, 26:353.

29. For a recent example, see "Ch'ongnyŏn i kŏrŏon sŭngni wa yŏnggwang ŭi 50-nyŏn," *Rodong sinmun*, May 25, 2005.

30. "Saram ŭi maŭm ŭl umjigil chul anŭn il'ggun i toeŏya," 454.

31. *Kim Il-sŏng wŏnsunim ŭn uri ŭi abŏji*, 110, 139, 160, 216, 223, etc.

32. Ibid., 21, 24-25.

33. Sin Chŏn, "Ch'oso e suryŏngnim i osyŏssne," lyrics on www1.big.or.jp /~jrldr/ korea/ c30.html.

34. Kim Chŏl-jin, O Kwang-ho, "Namjin e kil esŏ pyŏngsadŭl ŭi haenggun ŭl tolpwa chusinŭn Kim Il-sŏng wŏnsunim."; Kim In-hwan, Chŏng Yŏng-man, Ch'oi Sŏng-nyong, "P'yŏngyang wiwŏnhoe rŭl ch'aja chusin ŏbŏi suryŏngnim Kimil-sŏng tongji."

35. Chŏng Kyu-t'aek, "Han chŏnsa ŭi kŏn'gang ŭl nyŏmnyŏ hasiyŏ."

36. "Ŏdi e kyesimnikka, kŭriun changgunnim?"

37. *Kim Il-sŏng wŏnsunim ŭn uri ŭi abŏji*, 46.

38. Ibid., 273, 274, 275.

39. See the painting "Samjiyŏn ŭi saebyŏk kil," *Chosŏn yesul*, April 1982, 18.

40. See the picture on page 472 of *Pulmyŏl ŭi yŏngsang*, Pyongyang, 1992.

41. "Sarang ŭi yaksok," *Ch'ŏllima*, January 2005, 30.

42. *Yŏngsaeng*, 58.

43. The film: *Ch'inaehanŭn chidoja Kim Jŏng-il tongji ŭi t'ansaeng 50 tol*, 1992.

44. *Hirohito*, 27, 90, 195. *T'aeyang sungbae ŭi yŏngwŏnhan hwap'ok, 11*. A famous song in the North is entitled, "Long Live the Great Marshal Kim Il Sung" (Kim Il-sŏng taewŏnsu manmanse). See "Kim Jŏng-il ch'ongbisŏ inmin'gun hyŏpchudan konghun hapch'angdan ŭi kyŏngch'uk kongyŏn kwallam," Korean Central News Agency, July 28, 1998. For recent use of the word pattŭlda, see "Ilsim tangyŏl ŭi wiryŏk ŭl him igge kwasihan taechŏngch'i ch'ukchŏn," *Rodong sinmun*, October 19, 2005.

45. See for example, Armstrong, *The North Korean Revolution*, 222-223.

46. *The Denial of Death*, 224-225.

47. *Think No Evil*, 65.

Chapter Four

1. See the pictures "Chosŏn ŭi kŭngji" (1980) by Pak Chinsu et al, *Pukhan misul ŭi 50-nyŏn*, 89; "Samjiyŏn ŭi saebyŏk kil," *Chosŏn yesul*, April 1982, 18; "Na ŭi chŏnsadŭl i kidarigo isso," *Chosŏn yesul*, September 2005, front matter.

2. Summarized from the official encyclopaedia entry on Kim Jong Il in *Chosŏn taebaekkwa sajŏn*, 1:18-29; Choe In Su, *Kim Jong Il, the People's Leader*; *Kim Jŏng-il wŏnsunim hyŏngmyŏng ryŏksa: Kodŭng chunghakkyo: 4*, Pyongyang, 1999; "Brief History of Kim Jong Il," *Korean Central News Agency*, February 16, 2002.

3. Choe, *Kim Jong Il, the People's Leader*, 4.

4. Ibid., 50.

5. From a teacher's notes excerpted in the official biography: "Kim Jong Il does not want and even detests special favors." Ibid., 86.

6. *Yŏngsaeng*, 328-9.

7. The novel *Yŏngsaeng* shows Kim fretting constantly over his father's health.

8. Kim Kyu-hak, "Pulmyŏl ŭi chaguk ŭl chajŭsiŏ" (1982), *Pukhan misul ŭi 50-nyŏn*, 92.

9. Kang Kwan-ju, "Kim Jŏng-il tongji-rŭl chal pattŭrŏ nagaya hamnida," 12, 13, 10.

10. Ibid., 11-12.

11. See also "Chŏlse ŭi wiin ŭl ttarŭnŭn manmin ŭi hŭmmo," *Ch'ŏllima*, August 2004, 34.

12. Pak Il-myŏng, "Chŏnhwan," *Chosŏn munhak*, June 1999, 5-16.

13. Ibid., 5.

14. Ibid., 6.

15. Ibid., 6.

16. Ibid., 7.

17. Ibid.

18. Ibid., 8.

19. Ibid.

20. *Chŏnhwan*, 9.

21. See for example the television movie *Season's Greetings* (Ch'ukpok hamnida, 2001).

22. "Waejin samch'oso e kkaji chajaosiyŏ," *Chosŏn yesul*, October 2006, front matter; "Paengni mulgil e ŏrin pulmyŏl ŭi cha'uk," *Chosŏn yesul*, April 2005, front matter.

23. See the painting "Nagwŏn ŭi pompit," *Chosŏn yesul*, February 2006, front matter.

24. *T'aeyang sungbae ŭi yŏngwŏnhan hwap'ok*, 28, 29, 30, 31.

25. *Chŏnhwan*, 14.

26. "Kye Sun-hŭi sŏnsu rŭl wihan yŏnhoe," Korean Central News Agency, August 7, 2001.

27. "Kim Jong Il's Devoted Service to People," Korean Central News Agency, August 18, 2007.

28. Sim Chae-hun, "Uri ŏbŏi," *Chosŏn munhak*, December 2006, 4.

29. "Kŭp'um ŭl ttŏna mot sara sŏjŏngsi ŏmŏni rŭl ŭlp'ŭmyŏ," Korean Central News Agency, October 9, 2003.

30. See for example the television evening news of July 28, 2009.

31. Bix, 252.

32. "Hyŏngmyŏng ŭi sunoebu kyŏlsa ongwi harira," Korean Central Television, July 18, 2009.

33. Fenichel, quoted in Becker, 132.

Chapter Five

1. *Yŏngsaeng*, 439

2. Ibid., 252.

3. "Widaehan suhoja," *Ch'ŏllima*, December 2006, 9. In "Angnarhan miguk ŭi simni moryakchŏn," *Ch'ŏllima*, December 2007, 77, the USSR's collapse is likened to that of a "wet clay wall."

4. Ryu Jŏng-bong, Kim Ik-ha, "Che 13-ch'a P'yŏngyang ch'ukchŏn ŭi pam" (1989), *Pukhan misul ŭi 50-nyŏn*, 105.

5. A comparable picture, "Man'gyŏngdae ŭi kohyang chip," depicts a radiant Korean beauty showing Kim Il Sung's birthplace to an equally unsavory-looking group of foreigners. *T'aeyang sungbae ŭi yŏngwŏnhan hwap'ok* (2002), 82.

6. *Ch'ongddae*, 437, 462.

7. "Sŏnmul sogae," *Ch' ŏllima*, August 2004, 6-7. See also the film *Ch'inaehanŭn chidoja Kim Jŏng-il tongji ŭi t'ansaeng 50 tol*, made in 1992 to celebrate Kim Jong Il's fiftieth birthday; about ten of the film's seventy minutes are devoted to showing gifts newly received from abroad.

8. *Ryŏksa*, 254-255.

9. Ibid., 255.

10. "Yesul yŏnghwa <Nae gap on nara> (che 2, 3-bu) sisahoe," KCNA, July 27, 2009. The film was routinely discussed on the nightly news throughout the summer.

11. *Ryŏksa ŭi taeha*, 4, 8-9, 64, 208, 225, 316; Pak Dong-jin, *Sŭngnyangi mije ŭi choi'ak*; *Chosŏn taebaekkwa sajŏn*, 18:154.

12. See for example, Kim Su-ryŏn, "Sŭngnyangi ŭi ponsŏng ŭn pyŏnhaji annŭnda," *Adong munhak*, September 2003, 57.

13. Ri Sŭng-bŏm, "Nae ka chabŭn migungnom," *Chosŏn yesul*, May 2006, 47.

14. Sŏ, *Inmin i sanŭn mosŭp*, 1:97.

15. "The marks of the beast [in Japanese propaganda] were claws, fangs, animal hindquarters, sometimes a tail, sometimes small

horns…the quasi-religious demon or devil…was the dominant metaphor…A journalistic account…was accompanied by an illustration of Uncle Sam as a sharp-nailed, sharp-toothed clergyman with the tail of a fox." Dower, *War Without Mercy*, 244-245.

16. See the poster bearing the caption "Mije ŭi kyohwal han simnijŏk ch'aekdong ŭl kŏrŭm mada chitbusija," *Chosŏn munhak yesul nyŏn'gam: 2005*, 343.

17. *Sŭngnyangi*, 72.

18. *T'aeyang sungbae ŭi yŏngwŏnhan hwap'ok*, 56.

19. See for example the propaganda posters on the inside back covers of the January and February 1999 issues of the magazine *Ch'ŏllima*.

20. P'yŏngyang ŭi nunbora," In *Hŭk, ppuri*, 114-145.

21. Ibid., 134.

22. Ibid., 132.

23. Ibid., 144.

24. *Ryŏksa ŭi taeha*, 9. In Korean, the verb *mushi hada* has stronger connotations of contempt than the English word "to ignore"; it would not be wrong to translate it here as "to scorn."

25. The name change seems intended to spare Kang any awkwardness overseas.

26. *Ryŏksa ŭi taeha*, 61-62.

27. Ibid., 62.

28. Ibid., 63.

29. Ibid.

30. Ibid., 397.

31. Ibid.

32. *Ch'ŏngddae*, 432.

33. *Hyŏndae chosŏn mal sajŏn*, 1988, 1:1547; "Chegukchuŭi ŭi ch'imnyakchŏk ponsŏng ŭn chŏlttaero pyŏnhal su ŏpta," *Rodong sinmun*, January 11, 2000.

34. See the official praise for *Ryŏksa ŭi taeha* in the national yearbook *Chosŏn chungang nyŏn'gam: 1998*, 233.

35. "Chomi kibon habŭimun," *Chosŏn taebaekkwa sajŏn*, 17:545.

36. *Ryŏksa ŭi taeha*, 440.

37. Ibid., 487.

38. Ibid., 497.

39. Ibid., 320, 163-164, 443.

40. Szalontai, "You Have No Political Line," 97-98.

41. Ibid., 72-73. Bix, 326.

42. *Ch'ongddae*, 434.

43. Ibid., 107, 109, 268, 301.

44. The poster is on the inside back cover of the June 1998 issue of Chosŏn *munhak*.

45. A colorful poster depicting such a missile attack and bearing the caption, "Merciless punishment for US imperialism" (Mije ege mujabihan chingbŏl ŭl) was released by the KCNA to foreign news agencies on January 31, 2003.

46. See for example, the poster entitled "We will forever sweep from the earth anyone who messes with us," on the inside back cover of the March 1999 issue of *Chosŏn munhak*.

47. Sŏ, *Inmin i sanŭn mosŭp*, 1:99.

48. "Sŭngnyangi ŭi ponsŏng ŭn pyŏnhaji annŭnda," 57.

49. *Ch'ongddae*, 458.

50. Ibid., 442.

51. Ibid., 442.

52. "K'ŭllint'on miguk chŏn taet'ongnyŏng ŭi chosŏn pangmun kwa kwallyŏn han podo," KCNA, August 5, 2009.

53. Kim Ch'ang-hun, "Arirang hwasal," *Ch'ŏllima*, December 2007, 85.

54. "Chomun kibon habŭimun," *Chosŏn taebaekkwa sajŏn*, 17:545.

55. Kim Jong Il, "Mije nŭn uri wa han hanŭl ŭl igo sal su ŏmnŭn uri inmin ŭi ch'ŏlch'ŏnji wŏnssu imnida," a quote box printed on page 34 of the September 2006 issue of *Ch'ŏllima*.

56. "Ch'ŏn paekpae ro poksu hari," *Ch'ŏllima*, April 2005, 58.

57. Na Kyŏng-ho, "Ppalli ppalli k'ŏssŭmyŏn," excerpted in "Tongsim kwa hŭngmi," Kim Hae-wŏl, *Chosŏn munhak*, August 2004, 15.

58. Kim Yunsik, "Kiŏi poksu hari," *Chosŏn munhak*, March 1999, 80; see also "P'i kaps ŭl ch'ŏnpaekpae ro pada naerira," *Ch'ŏllima*, July 2006, 72.

59. This message is voiced, for example, in a "man on the street" type interview on the TV news of July 25, 2009.

60. The Korean original: "Uri ŭi chajonsim ŭl kŏndŭrinŭn cha, ŏdi e ittdŭn kyŏlp'an ŭl nael gŏsida."

61. Ellul, *Propaganda*, 73.

62. See for example, "<6.25 mije pandae t'ujaeng ŭi nal> P'yŏngyang-si kunjung taehoe chinhaeng," KCNA, June 25, 2009.

63. *Ch'ŏllima*, inside back cover, May 1999.

64. See the increase in anti-American articles and posters in *Ch'ŏllima* in 1998 and 1999, and the publication of *Jackals* (Sŭngnyangi, 1951) in *Chosŏn munhak, Ch'ŏngnyŏn munhak*, and *Ch'ŏllima* in August 2003.

Chapter Six

1. The classic old-style depiction of South Korea is Han Sŏl-ya's *Sarang* (1959), a thinly-veiled attempt to defame the Underwood family of missionary-educators. For the claim regarding Yankee shooting practice, see page 626.

2. Kim Il Sung, "Namchosŏn ŭn miguk ŭi wanjŏnhan singminjida," Kim Nam-ho, *Mannam*, Kim T'aek-wŏn, "Mije kangjŏm ha ŭi namchosŏn (kyoyukp'yŏn)."

3. "Iŏjin hyŏlmaek," *Chosŏn yesul*, January 2005, 62. "Paektusan sŏch'e rŭl ttarŭnŭn namnyŏk haksaengdŭl," *Chosŏn yesul*, November 2005, 37.

4. Kim Nam-ho, *Mannam* (2001), 129, 29, 60.

5. *Mannam*, 176.

6. Ibid., 359-360.

7. See Han Sŏrya, *Sarang*, 280, 317, 398, 449, 626; a school textbook quoted in Sŏ, *Inmin i sanŭn mosŭp, 1:96;* and the painting, "Ŏmma, nan an kallaeyo" (Mommy, I don't want to go!"), *Chosŏn yesul*, October 2007, 47. One painting shows a woman clinging to an airport fence, her baby-sling hanging empty from her back, while an American jet takes to the sky. The title: "You bastards! My boy…" *Chosŏn misul nyŏn'gam 1986*, 177. "Fight for Withdrawal of US Forces Urged in South Korea," Korean Central News Agency, September 14, 2007.

8. Ri, Sŏn'gun chŏngch'i esŏ pit'palch'inŭn chaju ŭi sinnyŏm," *Rodong sinmun*, April 5, 2005; "On kyŏre ka tŏk ŭl ponŭn sŏn'gun chŏngch'i," *Rodong sinmun*, November 2, 2006.

9. *Mannam*, 6-7.

10. Ibid., 71.

11. Ibid., 72.

12. *A choguk!* 377.

13. Ibid., 8.

14. *Mannam*, 5.

15. "Suddenly, Kim is 'cute,'" Ahn Mi-young, *Asia Times*, June 10, 2000.

16. *Mannam*, 20, 37, 208.

17. Ibid., 207.

18. Ibid., 214.

19. Ibid., 232.

20. *P'yŏnji*, 247.

21. *Pyŏl ŭi segye*, 2002, 5-6.

22. Ibid., 424.

23. See for example the illustration "Sinnyŏm," on the inside back cover of *Ch'ŏllima*, November 2006.

24. *P'yŏnji*, 220.

25. "Lee Myung Bak's Sycophancy Towards US and anti-DPRK Confrontation Hysteria Blasted," KCNA, April 1, 2008.

26. "Puk, pangsong p'yŏnjip hae 'namhan pich'am' sŏnjŏn," YTN, July 29, 2009.

Conclusion

1. A typical piece in this vein is Sigal and Namkung, "Setting a New Course with North Korea," *Washington Times*, October 19, 2008.

2. Kim Yon-se, "34% of Army Cadets Regard US as Main Enemy," *Korea Times*, April 6, 2008.

BIBLIOGRAPHY

"1952-nyŏn tang chungang wiwŏnhoe che 5-ch'a chŏnwŏnhoe ŭi ryŏksajŏk ŭiŭi." *Rodong sinmun*. December 19, 1962.

Ajami, Chaouki. *Juche: Theory and Application*. Pyongyang, 1978.

Alford, C. Fred. *Think No Evil: Korean Values in the Age of Globalization*. Ithaca, 1999.

"Angnalhan miguk ŭi simni moryakchŏn." *Ch'ŏllima*, December 2007, 77-78.

Armstrong, Charles. *The North Korean Revolution, 1945-1950*. Ithaca, 2003.

Becker, Ernest. *The Denial of Death*. New York, 1973.

Belke, Thomas J. *Juche: A Christian Study of North Korea's State Religion*. Bartlesville, OK, 1999.

Bell, Daniel. "The End of Ideology in the West. In *The End of Ideology Debate*. Edited by Chaim L. Waxman. 87-105. New York, 1968.

Bix, Herbert P. *Hirohito and the Making of Modern Japan*. New York, 2000.

Bratzke, Mike. *Kita Chōsen 'rakuen' no zangai*. Tokyo, 2003.

Brie, Horst. "Document No. 3: Report, GDR Embassy in the DPRK, 2 April 1965." Translated by Grace Leonard. In *Cold War International History Project Bulletin*, Issue 14/15 (Winter 2003-Spring 2004), 42-44.

Bright, Arthur. "Defectors: No Kim Jong Il Would Mean No Nuclear Threat." *The Christian Science Monitor*, October 18, 2006.

"Brilliant Life Dedicated to Country and Nation." Korean Central News Agency. July 6, 2007.

Burns, John F. "The Kim Dynasty's North Korea: A Nation Centered on One Family." *The New York Times*, July 9, 1985.

Ch'a Hak-che. "Sunnun'gil haech'isimyŏ chabajusin kongjang t'ŏjŏn." In *Inmindŭl sogesŏ*, 66:144-153. Pyongyang, 2005.

"Chegukchuŭi ŭi ch'imnyakchŏk ponsŏng ŭn chŏlttaero pyŏnhal su ŏpta." *Rodong sinmun*, January 11, 2000.

Chi Yŏng-hwan. "Oegugin bŏmjoi kŭpchŭng." *Chosŏn ilbo*, October 18, 2007.

Ch'inaehanŭn chidoja Kim Jŏng-il tongji ŭi t'ansaeng 50 tol (film, 70 minutes). Pyongyang, 1992.

Cho Kwan-ja. "'Minjok ŭi him' ŭl yongmanghan 'ch'inil naesyŏnŏlisŭt'ŭ' Yi Kwang-su." In *Haebang chŏnhusa ŭi chaeinsik*, 1: 524-555. Seoul, 2006.

Choe In Su. *Kim Jong Il, the People's Leader.* Pyongyang, 1983.

Ch'oi Chin-hŭi. "Puk ŭi yŏsŏng ch'abyŏl ŭn chongnyu to mant'a." Nkchosun. com. August 5, 2005.

Ch'oi Kang-suk. "Kangje tongwŏn chŏnpŏm omyŏng pŏsŏtta." *Sŏul sinmun,* November 13, 2006.

Ch'oi Kyŏng-hŭi. "Ch'inil munhak ŭi tto tarŭn ch'ŭngwi." *Haebang chŏnhusa ŭi chaeinsik,* 1:387-433.

Ch'oi Mun'il. "'Taminjok, tainjong sahoe' ronŭn minjok malsallon." *Rodong sinmun,* April 27, 2006.

Ch'oi Nam-sŏn. "Chŏllyŏk chŭnggang ch'onghu suho ŭi chillo." *Maeil sinbo,* March 7, 1945.

"Chŏlse ŭi wiin ŭl ttarŭnŭn manmin ŭi hŭmmo." *Ch'ŏllima,* August 2004, 34-35.

Chŏn In-gwang. "P'yŏngyang ŭi nunbora." In *Hŭk, ppuri,* 114-145. Pyongyang, 2007.

Chong Bong-uk. *A Handbook on North Korea.* Seoul, 1988.

Chŏng Ki-jong. *Ryŏksa ŭi taeha.* Pyongyang, 2000.

————————. *Pyŏl ŭi segye.* Pyongyang, 2006.

Chosŏn chŏnsa. Volume 23. Pyongyang, 1981.

Chosŏn mal sajŏn. Pyongyang, 1962.

Chosŏn munhak t'ongsa. Pyongyang, 1959.

Chosŏn taebaekkwa sajŏn. Pyongyang, 1999-2000.

Clark, Katerina. *The Soviet Novel: History as Ritual.* Chicago and London. 1981.

Cleaver, Eldridge. *Soul on Fire.* London, 1979.

Clifford, Mark. "A Nation of Famine and Adulation: Letter from Pyongyang." *Business Week,* December 18, 2000.

Connor, Walker. *Ethnonationalism: The Quest for Understanding.* Princeton, 1994.

Cornell, Erick. "An Oddly Troublesome Couple." *The Daily Times* (Australia), January 29, 2003.

Cumings, Bruce. *Korea's Place in the Sun: A Modern History.* (Updated Edition.) New York, 1997.

————————. *North Korea: Another Country.* New York, 2004.

————————. *Origins of the Korean War: The Roaring of the Cataract, 1947-1950.* Princeton, 1990.

————————. "We look at it and see ourselves." *The London Review of Books,* December 15, 2005.

Demick, Barbara. "North Korea Seeks End to UN Aid." *The Los Angeles Times,* September 19, 2005.

Dower, John W. *War Without Mercy: Race and Power in the Pacific War.* New York, 1986.

Ellul, Jacques. *Propaganda: The Formation of Men's Attitudes.* New York, 1973.

Fifield, Anna. "South Korea blocks pro-North websites." *Financial Times,* March 26, 2007.

Gabroussenko, Tatiana. *Soldiers on the Cultural Front.* Unpublished manuscript.

"God of Present Century Published." Korean Central News Agency, March 10, 2000.

Good Friends. "Human Rights in North Korea and the Food Shortage: A Comprehensive Report on North Korean Human Rights Issues." Seoul, 2005.

Gourevitch, Philip. "Letter from North Korea: Alone in the Dark." *The New Yorker,* September 18, 2003.

Gross, Daniel. "Thanks for the Cheap Gas, Mr. Hitler! How Nazi Germany and Apartheid South Africa Perfected One of the World's Most Exciting New Fuel Sources." *Slate,* October 23, 2006.

Haggard, Stephen, and Noland, Marcus. *Famine in North Korea: Markets, Aid and Reform.* New York, 2007.

Han Pyŏng-gu. "Pukhan ŭi sinmun." In *Pukhan ŭi ŏllon,* 85-138. Seoul, 1989.

Han Sŏr-ya. *Hyŏllo.* In *Han Sŏr-ya sŏnjip.* Pyongyang, 1960-1962. 8:3-31.

⸺. "Kim Il-sŏng changgun kwa minjok munhwa ŭi paltchŏn. In *Han Sŏr-ya sŏnjip.* Pyongyang, 1960-1962. 14:23-33.

⸺. *Man'gyŏngdae.* In *Han Sŏr-ya sŏnjip.* Pyongyang, 1960-1962. 9:362-491.

⸺. *Nammae.* In *Han Sŏr-ya sŏnjip.* Pyongyang, 1960-1962. 8:156-241.

⸺. "Pabo k'ongk'ŭl." In *Han Sŏr-ya sŏnjip.* Pyongyang, 1960-1962. 14:264-305.

⸺. *Ryŏksa.* In *Han Sŏr-ya sŏnjip.* Pyongyang, 1960-1962. 9:1-360.

⸺. *Sarang.* In *Han Sŏr-ya sŏnjip.* Pyongyang, 1960-1962. Vol. 12.

⸺. *Sŭngnyangi.* Tokyo, 1954.

⸺. *Ttangk'ŭ 214ho.* In *Han Sŏr-ya sŏnjip.* Pyongyang, 1960-1962. 8:550-596.

Han Ung-bin. *A, choguk!* Pyongyang, 2004.

Han Yun. *Ssiat.* Pyongyang, 1992.

Harden, Blaine. "All Nuclear Efforts Disclosed, North Korea Says," *Washington Post*, January 5, 2008.

Ho Hyŏn-ch'an. *Han'guk yŏnghwa 100-nyŏn.* Seoul, 2000.

Hong Sŏk-chung, *Hwang Jin'i*, Seoul, 2003.

Hwang Chang-yŏp. *Hoegorok.* Seoul, 2006.

Hwang Ryŏng'a. "Tasi toraon taramchui." *Adong munhak*, December 2005, 42-45.

"Ilsim tangyŏl ŭi wiryŏk ŭl him'igge kwasihan taechŏngch'i ch'ukchŏn." *Rodong sinmun*, October 19, 2005.

Inmindŭl sok esŏ. Volume 66. Pyongyang, 2005.

Judt, Tony. *Postwar: A History of Europe Since 1945.* New York, 2005.

Kang Ch'ŏr-wŏn. "3-dae rŭl iŏ angyŏjusin sarang kwa ŭnjŏng." In *Inmindŭl sok esŏ*, 66:167-193. Pyongyang, 2005.

Kang Hyŏn-du. "Pukhan ŭi pangsong." In *Pukhan ŭi ŏllon*, 141-182. Seoul, 1989.

Kang Kwan-ju. "Kim Jŏng-il tongji rŭl chal pattŭrŏ nagaya hamnida." In *Inmindŭl sok esŏ*, 66:1-14. Pyongyang, 2005.

Kang, Thomas Hosuck. *Why the North Koreans Behave as They Do.* Washington, DC, 1994.

Kelleher, Theresa. "Confucianism." In *Women in World Religions, edited by Arvind Sharma*, 135-159. Albany, 1987.

Kenez, Peter. *The Birth of the Propaganda State: Soviet Methods of Mass Mobilization: 1917-1929.* New York, 1985.

Kim Ch'ang-hun. "Arirang hwasal." *Chŏllima*, December 2007, 85.

Kim Ch'ŏl. (ROK) "Mollakhanŭn sinsaeng – 'Manju ŭi kkum kwa 'nonggun' ŭi odok." In *Haebang chŏnhusa ŭi chaeinsik*. 1:479-523.

Kim Ch'ŏl. (DPRK) "Ŏmŏni." *Ch'ŏllima*, October 2005, 12-13.

Kim Hae-wŏl. "Tongsim kwa hŭngmi." *Chosŏn munhak*, August 2004, 14-18.

Kim Il Sung. (Kim Il-sŏng.) "Chŏnch'e chakka yesulgadŭl ege." In *Kim Il-sŏng sŏnjip*, 3:238-251. Pyongyang, 1954.

_____. "Chosŏn minjujuŭi inmin konghwaguk esŏ ŭi sahoejuŭi kŏnsŏl kwa Namchosŏn hyŏngmyŏng e taehayŏ." *Kim Ilsŏng chŏjak sŏnjip*, 4:195-240. Pyongyang, 1968.

_____. "Chosŏn rodongdang che 4-ch'a taehoe esŏ han chungang wiwŏnhoe saŏp ch'onghwa pogo." *Kim Il-sŏng chŏjak sŏnjip*, 3:60-203. Pyongyang, 1968.

_____. "Kangsŏ-gun tang saŏp chido esŏ ŏdŭn kyohun e taehayŏ." *Kim Il-sŏng chŏjak sŏnjip*,1:63-68. Pyongyang, 1967.

_____. "Kangsŏ-gun tang saŏp chido esŏ ŏdŭn kyohun e taehayŏ: Chosŏn rodongdang chungang wiwŏnhoe sangmu wiwŏnhoe hwaktae hoeŭi esŏ han yŏnsŏl, 1960-nyŏn 2-wŏl 23-il." *Kim Il-sŏng chŏjak sŏnjip*. Pyongyang, 1968. 2: 505-542.

_____. "Munhwa wa yesul ŭn inmin ŭl wihan kŏs ŭro teoŏya handa." *Kim Il-sŏng sŏnjip*, 1:96-104. Pyongyang, 1955.

_____. "Namchosŏn ŭn Miguk ŭi wanjŏnhan singminji ida." Pyongyang, 2000.

_____. "Sahoejuŭi hyŏngmyŏng ŭi hyŏndangye e issŏsŏ tang mit' kukka saŏp ŭi myŏt kaji munjedŭl e taehayŏ." In *Kim Il-sŏng chŏjak sŏnjip*, 1:532-559. Pyongyang, 1967.

_____. "Sasang saŏp esŏ kyojojuŭi wa hyŏngsikchuŭi rŭl t'oech'i hago chuch'e rŭl hwangnip halte taehayŏ." In *Kim Il-sŏng chŏjak sŏnjip*, 1:560-585. Pyongyang, 1967.

_____. "Uri tang ŭi chuch'e sasang kwa konghwaguk chŏngbu ŭi taenaewoe chŏngch'aek ŭi myŏt kaji munje e taehayŏ." In *Kim Il-sŏng chŏjakchip*, 27:390-402. Pyongyang, 1984.

Kim Il-sŏng wŏnsunim ŭn uri ŭi abŏji. Pyongyang, 1981.

Kim Jong Il (Kim Jŏng-il). "Mije nŭn uriwa han hanŭl ŭl igo sal su ŏmnŭn uri inmin ŭi ch'ŏlch'ŏnji wŏnssu imnida." *Ch'ŏllima*, September 2006, 34.

_____. "Sahoejuŭi hyŏnsil ŭl panyŏnghan hyŏngmyŏngjŏk yŏnghwa rŭl tŏ manhi ch'angjak haja," *Kim Jŏng-il sŏnjip*, 2:75-120. Pyongyang, 1993.

_____. "Saram ŭi maŭm ŭl umjigil chul anŭn il'ggun i toeŏya handa," *Kim Jŏng-il sŏnjip*. Vol. 1. Pyongyang, 1992. 448-456.

"Kim Jŏng-il ch'ongbisŏ inmin'gun hyŏpchudan konghun hapch'angdan ŭi kyŏngch'uk kongyŏn kwallam." Korean Central News Agency, July 28, 1998.

Kim Jŏng-il wŏnsunim hyŏngmyŏng ryŏksa: Kodŭng chunghakkyo: 4, Pyongyang, 1999.

Kim Jong Suk, Mother of Korea. Pyongyang, 1997.

Kim Nam-ho. *Mannam.* Pyongyang, 2001.

Kim Sang-sun (ed). *T'aeyang sungbae ŭi yŏngwŏnhan hwap'ok.* Pyongyang, 2002.

Kim Sa-ryang. "Uri nŭn irŏk'e igyŏtta," in *Kim Sa-ryang sŏnjip.* Pyongyang, 1955. 341-369.

Kim Su-ryŏn. "Sŭngnyangi ŭi ponsŏng ŭn pyŏnhaji annŭnda," *Adong munhak,* September 2003, 57.

Kim T'aek-wŏn. *Mije kangjŏm ha ŭi Namchosŏn: kyoyukp'yŏn.* Pyongyang, 1963.

Kim Yon-se. "34% of Army Cadets Regard US as Main Enemy." *Korea Times,* April 6, 2008.

Kimura, Mitsuhiko. "Pasijŭm esŏ kongsanjuŭi ro." In Pak Chi-hyang, et al, *Haebang chŏnhusa ŭi chaeinsik.* Seoul, 2006. 1:737-764.

Kristol, Irving. "Keeping Up With Ourselves." In: *The End of Ideology Debate.* Edited by Chaim Waxman. 106-115. New York, 1968.

Ku Sang-mo. (Ed.) *Pukhan chumin ŭi ilsang saenghwal kwa taejung munha.* Seoul, 2003.

"K'ŭllint'on miguk chŏn taet'ongnyŏng ŭi Chosŏn pangmun kwa kwallyŏn han podo." Korean Central News Agency, August 5, 2009.

"Kŭp'um ŭl ttŏna mot sara sŏjŏngsi ŏmŏni rŭl ŭlp'ŭmyŏ." Korean Central News Agency, October 9, 2003.

"Kukchejŏk myŏnmo katchwŏganŭn P'yŏngyang yŏnghwach'ukchŏn." Nkchosun.com, September 20, 2004.

"Kunindŭl ŭi mayak changsa. Haegun kyŏngbijŏng ŭro mulgŏn olmgyŏ." *Chosun ilbo,* March 21, 2008.

"Kunmin ilch'i ro sŭngni rŭl haja." *Rodong sinmun,* May 26, 1998.

"Kwan'gae kongsajang ŭl hyŏnji jido hayŏjusinŭn Kim Il-sŏng tongji." *Chosŏn yesul,* March 1982, front matter.

Lankov, Andrei. *Crisis in North Korea: The Failure of De-Stalinization, 1956.* Honolulu, 2004.

—————————. *From Stalin to Kim Il Sung: The Formation of North Korea, 1945-1960.* New Brunswick, New Jersey, 2002.

Martin, Bradley. *Under the Loving Care of the Fatherly Leader: North Korea and the Kim Dynasty.* New York, 2004.

McCormack, Gavin. "Book Talk." ABC Radio National, March 1, 2003.

Minjok munje yŏn'guso. *Singminji Chosŏn kwa chŏnjaeng misul.* Seoul, 2004.

Myers, Brian. "Concerted Front." *The Wall Street Journal*, December 24, 2006.

——————. *Han Sŏrya and North Korean Literature: The Failure of Socialist Realism in the DPRK*. Ithaca, 1994.

——————. "Ideology as Smokescreen: North Korea's Juche Thought." *Acta Koreana*, December 2008, 161-182.

——————. "Mother of All Mothers: The Leadership Secrets of Kim Jong Il." *The Atlantic Monthly*, September 2004.

——————. "Mother Russia: Soviet Characters in North Korean Fiction," in *Korean Studies* 16: 82-93.

——————. "North Korean Literature and the Food Shortage: Pak Il Myeong's Short Story Transition (Cheonhwan). In: *2002-nyŏn, kyŏkbyŏn hanŭn han bando chŏngse ŭi punsŏk kwa pyŏngka*, 25-37. Seoul, 2002.

——————. "Rethinking Notions of a 'Confucian' Personality Cult in North Korea." In *Kim Dong-gyu kyosu hŏnjŏng nonmunjip*. Seoul, 2004.

——————. "The Watershed That Wasn't: Re-Evaluating Kim Il Sung's "Juche Speech" of 1955." *Acta Koreana*, January 2006, 89-115.

"Myŏngŏn haesŏl: 'Uri ŭi sahoejuŭi choguk ŭn Kim Il-sŏng choguk imyŏ uri minjok ŭn Kim Il-sŏng minjogimnida.'" *Ch'ŏngnyŏn munhak*, March 2004, 18.

"Nagwŏn ŭi pompit." *Chosŏn yesul*, February 2006, front matter.

Namkung, K.A., Sigal, Leon V. "Setting a New Course With North Korea." *Washington Times*, October 19, 2008.

Noland, Marcus. *Avoiding the Apocalypse: The Future of the Two Koreas*. Washington, DC, 2000.

"Nuga pwado choŭn tchalbŭn mŏri hyŏngt'ae." *Ch'ŏllima*, January 2005, 97.

Oh, Kongdan; Hassig, Ralph C. *North Korea through the Looking Glass*. Washington, DC, 2000.

"On kyŏre ka tŏk ŭl ponŭn sŏn'gun chŏngch'i." *Rodong sinmun*, November 2, 2006.

Paek Po-hŭm, Song Sang-wŏn. *Yŏngsaeng*. Pyongyang, 1997.

Paek Ŭn-p'al. *P'yŏnji*. Pyongyang, 2005.

"Paektu san sŏch'e rŭl ttarunŭn namnyŏk haksaengdŭl." In *Chosŏn yesul*, November 2005, 37.

Paige, Glenn D.; Lee, Dong Jun. "The Post-War Politics of Communist Korea." *North Korea Today*. Edited by Robert A. Scalapino. New York, 1963. 17-29.

Pak Chi-hyang. Kim Ch'ŏl, Kim I-ryŏng, Yi Yŏng-hun. *Haebang chŏnhusa ŭi chaeinsik.* In 2 volumes. Seoul, 2006.

Pak Tong-jin. *Sŭngnyangi mije ŭi choiʾak.* Pyongyang, 1983.

Pak Il-myŏng. *Chŏnhwan. Chosŏn munhak,* June 1999, 5-16.

Pang Chae-sun. "Choguk ŭi pʾum." *Ch'ŏllima,* August 2004, 70-71.

Pauer, Erich. (Ed.) *Japan's War Economy.* London, 1999.

Pfabigan, Alfred. *Schlaflos in Pjöngjang.* Vienna, 1986.

"P'ikaps-ŭl ch' ŏnpaekpae ro padanaerira." *Ch' ŏllima,* July 2006, 72.

Pocha, Jehangir S. "Choreographing Success in North Korea." *The Boston Globe,* October 30, 2005.

"Puk, pangsong p'yŏnjip hae 'Namhan pich'am' sŏnjŏn." YTN. July 29, 2009.

Pulmyŏl ŭi yŏngsang. Pyongyang, 1992.

Ramstad, Evan. "Gulags, Nukes and a Water Slide: Citizen Spies Lift North Korea's Veil." *The Wall Street Journal,* May 22, 2009.

Ri Sŏk-ch'ŏl. "Sŏn'gun chŏngch'i esŏ pit'palch'inŭn chaju ŭi sinnyŏm." *Rodong sinmun,* April 5, 2005.

"*Rodong sinmun* chŏngnon 'Kŭp'um ttŏna mot sara': sŏjŏngsi Ŏmŏni rŭl ŭlp'ŭmyŏ." Korean Central News Agency, October 9, 2003.

"*Rodong sinmun* on Korean People's Inexhaustible Mental Power." Korean Central News Agency, January 29, 2008.

"*Rodong sinmun* on Role Played by WPK as Mother Party." Korean Central News Agency, December 14, 2007.

"Samjiyŏn ŭi saebyŏk kil." *Chosŏn yesul,* April 1982, 18.

"Sarang ŭi yaksok." *Ch'ŏllima,* January 2005, 30.

Schäfer, Bernd. "North Korean 'Adventurism' and China's Long Shadow, 1966-1972," Working paper #44, Cold War International History Project, Washington DC, October 2004.

_____. "Weathering the Sino-Soviet Conflict: The GDR and North Korea, 1949-1989." *Cold War International History Project Bulletin.* Issue 14/15 (Winter 2003-Spring 2004). 25-38.

Schurmann, Franz. *Ideology and Organization in Communist China.* Second and enlarged edition. Berkeley and Los Angeles, 1966.

Shen Zhihua. "Sino-North Korean Conflict and its Resolution during the Korean War." *Cold War International History Project Bulletin,* Issue 14-15, Winter 2003-Spring 2004, 9-38.

Shin, Gi-Wook. *Ethnic Nationalism in Korea: Genealogy, Politics and Legacy.* Stanford, California, 2006.

Sim Chae-hun. "Uri ŏbŏi." *Chosŏn munhak*, December 2006, 4.

Sin Chu-hyŏn. "Kim Il-sŏng, ch'inil int'elli to kanbu ro tŭngyong hetta." www.dailynk.com, September 16, 2005.

Sin Hyŏng-gi. "Sinin'gan – haebang chikhu pukhan munhak i kŭryŏnaen tongwŏn ŭi hyŏngsang." In *Haebang chŏnhusa ŭi chaeinsik*, 1:733-734.

Sŏ Kwang-sŏn. "Yŏnp'ung chunghakkyo e saegyŏjin sarang ŭi chŏnsŏl." In *Inmindŭl sok esŏ*, 66:154-166.

Sŏ Man-sul. "Ŏmŏni choguk e tŭrinŭn kŭl." *Rodong sinmun*, September 17, 2003.

Sŏ Sŏng-nyong. "Pom hanŭl." *Chŏngnyŏn munhak*, October 1990, 8-15.

Song Min-ho. *Iljemal amhŭkki munhak yŏn'gu*, Seoul, 1989.

Sternhell, Zeev. "Fascist Ideology." In *Fascism: A Reader's Guide*. Edited by Walter Laqueur. 315-376. Berkeley and Los Angeles, 1976.

Szalontai, Balázs. *Kim Il Sung in the Khrushchev Era: Soviet-DPRK Relations and the Roots of North Korean Despotism, 1953-1964*. Washington, DC, 2005.

_____. "'You Have No Political Line of Your Own': Kim Il Sung and the Soviets, 1953-1964. *Cold War International History Project Bulletin*. Issue 14/15 (Winter 2003/Spring 2004), 87-103.

"Taedamhan konggyŏk chŏngsin ŭro kyŏngje kangguk kŏnsŏl ŭl wihan ch'ongjin'gun ŭl himigge tagŭch'ija." *Rodong sinmun*, May 22, 2008.

Taejung chŏngchi yong'ŏ sajŏn. Pyongyang, 1959.

Turney-High, Harry Holbert. *Primitive War: Its Practice and Concepts*. Second Edition. Columbia, 1991.

"Two Koreas' Top Brass Resort to Racist Mudslinging." *Chosun Ilbo* (English Language Edition), May 17, 2006.

Weathersby, Kathryn. "Korea, 1949-50: To Attack, or Not to Attack? Stalin, Kim Il Sung, and the Prelude to War." *Cold War International History Project Bulletin*, Issue 5 (1995), 1-9.

Weber, Eugen. "Revolution? Counterrevolution? What Revolution?" *Fascism: A Reader's Guide*. Berkeley and Los Angeles, 1978. 435-467.

"Widaehan ŏmŏni tang." *Rodong sinmun*, October 3, 2003.

"Widaehan suhoja." *Ch'ŏllima*, December 2006, 9.

Widaehan suryŏng Kim Il-lsŏng tongji ŭi pulmyŏl ŭi hyŏngmyŏng ŏpchŏk 18: haewoe kyop'o munje ŭi pit'nanŭn haegyŏl. Pyongyang, 1999.

"Wihŏmhan pul changnan." *Ch'ŏllima*, June 1998, 59.

Wiseman, Paul. "North Koreans Savor Taste of Open Marketplace." *USA Today*, February 19, 2009.

Yang, Key P., Chee, Chang-boh. "The North Korean Educational System: 1945 to Present." *North Korea Today*. Edited by Robert A. Scalapino. New York. 1963. 125-140.

Yi Ch'un-jin. *Anna*. In *Koji ŭi yŏngungdŭl: Yi Ch'un-jin tanpyŏnjip*. 5-39. Pyongyang, 1960.

Yi Ku-yŏl. *Pukhan misul 50 nyŏn*. Seoul, 2001.

Yi U-yŏng. *Pukhan ŭi chabonjuŭi insik pyŏnhwa*. Seoul, 2000.

Yi Yŏng-hun. "Wae tashi haebang chŏnhusa inga." *Haebang chŏnhusa ŭi chaeinsik*. 1:25-63. Seoul, 2006.

Zagoria, David S. "Some Comparisons Between the Russian and the Chinese Models." In *Communist Strategies in Asia: A Comparative Analysis of Governments and Parties*. 11-33. New York, 1963.